# The Prairie School Tradition

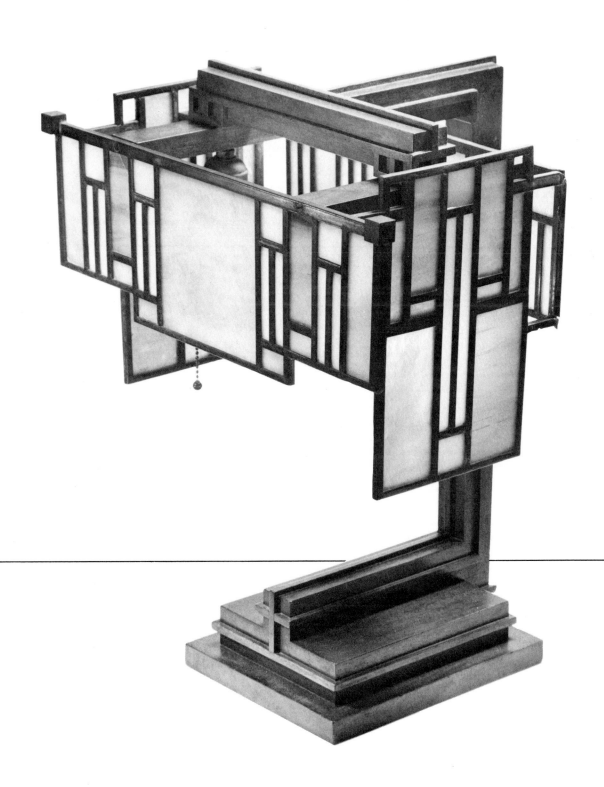

# The Prairie School

THE PRAIRIE ARCHIVES OF THE MILWAUKEE ART CENTER
EDITED BY BRIAN A. SPENCER, AIA

# Tradition

WHITNEY LIBRARY OF DESIGN
AN IMPRINT OF WATSON-GUPTILL PUBLICATIONS/NEW YORK

First published 1979 in the United States and Canada by Whitney Library of Design,
an imprint of Watson-Guptill Publications,
a division of Billboard Publications, Inc.,
1515 Broadway, New York, N.Y. 10036

**Library of Congress Cataloging in Publication Data**
Milwaukee. Art Center. Prairie Archives.
   The Prairie school tradition.
   Bibliography: p.
   Includes index.
   1. Prairie school (Architecture) 2. Architecture,
Modern—20th century—Middle West. I. Spencer, Brian A.,
1942-      II. Title.
NA722.M54 1979      720'.977      79-321
ISBN 0-8230-7432-3

Manufactured in U.S.A.

First Printing, 1979

The Prairie Archives of the Milwaukee Art Center gratefully acknowledges
The National Endowment for the Arts' Visiting Specialist Program, a federal
agency created by an act of Congress in 1965, The Wisconsin Arts Board,
The Affiliated State Art Agencies of the Upper Midwest, The Saltzstein
Foundation, The Edgar J. Kaufmann Foundation, The George L.N. Meyer
Family Foundation, The Caroline Draves Foundation, The James A. Taylor
Family Foundation, and others, who prefer to remain anonymous, for their
generous commitments and assistance to the exhibition.

We are indebted to the Associated General Contractors of Greater Milwaukee for their generous support in providing for the photographic
documentation of "An American Architecture: Its Roots, Growth and Horizons," the basis of this book.

Frontispiece
Table lamp, art glass with walnut base
Anonymous  no date
20 × 16½ × 12" (51 × 42 × 31 cm)
Courtesy Bertrand and Margaret Goderstad

# CONTENTS

# ACKNOWLEDGMENTS

Acknowledgment of a very special nature must be given to the Milwaukee Art Center and its Board of Trustees which provided for the development of an architectural program as part of the focus of the institution. My belief is that it will provide an exciting and vital area of study for the student, scholar, architectural profession, and the general public.

As ideas for the exhibition "An American Architecture: Its Roots, Growth and Horizons" developed, I felt there would be no great problems with mounting the exhibition and preparing the subsequent publication. But I soon became aware of the many requirements for such an undertaking. I want to express my gratitude to the Milwaukee Art Center's Director, Gerald Nordland, and to I. Michael Danoff, Associate Director, for their support and guidance as well as to the staff members of the Milwaukee Art Center and the number of individuals who contributed their advice and assistance. Particular mention should be made of the efforts of Marilyn Drucker, J. Eugene Felsch, Jane Glasberg, Rosalie Goldstein, and Lawrence Stadler.

In addition, acknowledgment should be made for the efforts and contributions of Sarah Bodine and Susan Davis as well as the entire staff at the Whitney Library of Design.

A very special acknowledgment is made to T. Victoria Hansen for her continued assistance—truly an associate.

Deep appreciation, for tolerating the long and necessary hours in undertaking this entire project, goes to my wife, Pam.

For myself, and on behalf of the Prairie Archives and the Milwaukee Art Center, I would like to extend a most grateful thank you to the architects, institutions, and private collectors whose loans to the exhibition and for this book made the idea a reality.

# FOREWORD

BY GERALD NORDLAND

*The Prairie School Tradition* is based on a major architectural exhibition held at the Milwaukee Art Center in the fall of 1977. The exhibition, "An American Architecture: Its Roots, Growth and Horizon," inaugurated the Milwaukee Art Center's Prairie Archives Program, one designed to implement the institution's philosophy of integrating architecture into the fine arts.

Architecture is an influential but daily art and deserves study and documentation as an important commitment of the Milwaukee Art Center. We have the responsibility of insuring that the architectural heritage of the Midwest is preserved, for it is the art of building design that gives additional meaning to the visual and decorative arts. The Prairie school is the first genuine American architecture that did not imitate past styles, but rather set the pattern for indigenious architectural design. This pattern is not defined or closed. It is a continuing ideal that is perpetuated by architects, designers, and artists who today practice it with the concern that the land, the building, and man coexist in harmony.

# INTRODUCTION

"With all our freedom, we do not tolerate oddness. We in-
sist, in this country, upon everything's being cut to one
pattern."

Reverend William Henry Furness (father of Frank Furness)
Fourth Annual Convention American Institute of Architects
Philadelphia, Pennsylvania   9 November 1870

Contrary to this statement by the Reverend Furness, America has encouraged and fostered innovative genius and
nonconformity, even though it has not always recognized its
importance. Our built environment—architecture—is a case
in point. Throughout the first century of our nation's history,
emphasis was placed on gaining freedom and defining
what American democracy should be. Architectural styles
reflected the past, both in a technical sense and in terms of
our traditional ties to the culture and architecture of Western
Europe. Technically, men built with the tools, materials, and
craftsmanship brought with their immigration. Regarding
style, there was a similar continuation of tradition and bor-
rowing of patterns. For example, Thomas Jefferson's revival
of the architecture of the Roman Republic became a sym-
bolic and stylistic model for virtually every type of public
building. In the early 19th century, a vogue for the Gothic
saw spires and intricate tracery ornament inspired by the
great cathedrals of Europe graced even the most humble
wooden frame structures. Throughout the 19th century, revival styles flourished, growing more eclectic as various
styles and their motifs were mixed.

But the 19th century also saw many changes taking
place in America. With the political and economic success
of the new nation, the desire for a greater degree of cultural
independence also developed. Given an expanding technology, prosperity, and a climate which supported free-
thinkers and original ideas, a few early architects began to
see possibilities for experimentation and expansion beyond
the dictates of European architectural styles. It is this development, this movement based on defining and creating an
indigenous American architecture, which was the subject of
the Prairie Archives of the Milwaukee Art Center exhibition:
"An American Architecture: Its Roots, Growth and Horizons," (October 21, 1977, to January 8, 1978). This movement ventured beyond the mere creation of a new style,
embodying an approach to design which recognized, and
continues to recognize, the ideals of American democracy,
responsive to the social, cultural, and technological changes
in a rapidly moving society.

It should come as no surprise that the center for this
phenomena was the Midwest, and particularly Chicago. Far
removed from East Coast ties to Europe and conservatism,
Chicago was a city of booming industrial and technological
growth from the middle of the 19th century onward. The
need for buildings of all types was tremendous, resources
were plentiful, and clients were often self-made men who
were not opposed to innovation.

Although the major developments of the "new architecture" were to take place in the Midwest, the earliest roots of
the movement can be traced to the experiments of two architects who began practicing architecture in the East. Frank
Furness (1839-1912), son of the free-thinking Reverend William Henry Furness, began to experiment with forms of stylized ornament which were based on organic motifs rather
than on historical forms. In his work, beautiful patterns
based on nature began to appear in gables, on capitals,
and in other places which had previously been reserved for
more traditional styles of decoration. Henry Hobson Richardson (1836-1886), who had studied briefly with Furness in
Philadelphia, went even further than Furness by experiment-
ing with the fundamental ideas of space and massing.
While still dependent on a heavy Romanesque style for several of his buildings, his was a new treatment which ac-
knowledged rather than attempted to disguise mass and
solid forms. His Marshall Field Wholesale Store uses re-
peated arches to give a sense of unity to the building, while
at no time suggesting a Romanesque building or anything

other than one of the world's early skyscrapers. In other works, Richardson's use of natural materials (uncut rather than polished stone) and his blending of architectural forms with the natural environment show a sensitivity to the natural setting which will remain a key concern in this new approach.

Richardson's later buildings in Chicago served as an important source of inspiration for Louis H. Sullivan (1856-1924), who has often been called "the father of modern American architecture." Sullivan's early partnership with Dankmar Adler (1844-1900), an architect/engineer self-taught in the latest technological possibilities, produced classic contemporary designs such as the Transportation Building for the Chicago World's Colombian Exposition of 1893, the Auditorium Building, and several early skyscrapers. Throughout his career, Sullivan promoted the ideal of a design process which "grows from within," and even his later works—a series of small "jewel-box" banks scattered throughout the Midwest—represent a high point in the integration of form and function. His highly individualized ornament, which some have seen as being reminiscent of the flowing Art Nouveau style, served to emphasize and not disguise the function.

Louis H. Sullivan's importance in the movement toward a modern American approach to architecture can only partly be judged by his buildings. Far more significant was the role he played as a philosopher and teacher. Eloquently expressed in his writings and lectures, Sullivan's ideas were also transmitted to the next generation through the young people gathered around him who came to work in his architectural office. Most important and well-known of these young men was Frank Lloyd Wright, who became a draftsman in Sullivan's studio in 1888.

The role played by Frank Lloyd Wright (1867-1959) in the development of modern American architecture cannot be overstated. It was Wright who was able to give the philosophy of Louis H. Sullivan its highest architectural expression. As his own ideas developed and matured, Wright's philosophy of "organic architecture" stressed an honest use of materials, a respect for the natural environment, an integration of structural and aesthetic beauty, and above all a sensitivity to human life. As he stated: ". . . architecture which is really architecture proceeds from the ground, and somehow the terrain; the native industrial conditions, the nature of materials and the purpose of the building must inevitably determine the form and character of any good building." The first manifestation of this ideal came as early as the 1890s, with the creation of what is now described as the "Prairie style." Echoing the flat terrain of the Midwestern prairies, Wright's early work stressed horizontal planes, with bands of windows and low, wide rooflines. Natural wood, brick, and stone were used both inside and out, and every attempt was made to integrate interior and exterior space. To Frank Lloyd Wright, the integrity of architecture was not defined merely by its walls and roof, but by the space within. It is with justification that, as an architect, Wright is credited with "the destruction of the box."

While it is necessary to focus on the genius of Frank Lloyd Wright, it is equally important to examine the growth of the early contemporaries and students of what Wright called the "New School of the Midwest." Whether working directly with Wright or not, all were guided by his principles as well as his forms. George Grant Elmslie (1871-1952) worked with Wright in the offices of both Joseph Lyman Silsbee and Louis H. Sullivan. The influence of Sullivan's style of ornament as well as Wright's concept of space is shown in Elmslie's work for the great master and his later partnership with William Gray Purcell (1880-1964) and George Feick, Jr. (1881-1945). Parker N. Berry (1888-1918) was one of the last draftsmen to work for Louis Sullivan. His premature death only allows speculation about how his style might have developed. Walter Burley Griffin (1876-1937) and Francis Barry Byrne (1883-1967) were among the several young designers who worked in Wright's early Oak Park studio, each interpreting Wright's principles and bringing variety to the movement. Other architects, such as Percy Dwight Bentley (1885-1968), never studied with either Sullivan or Wright, although Bentley absorbed the concepts of these architects while living in Chicago. Bentley then returned to La Crosse, Wisconsin, to create outstanding examples in the Prairie idiom in relative isolation.

The independent collaborators and craftsmen who helped to complete the total harmony of the design were as important as the circle of architects gathered around Frank Lloyd Wright. These were the glassmakers, sculptors, potters, furniture makers, and landscape architects who were able to grasp the spirit of the Prairie ideal and transformed every detail of the interior and exterior in keeping with it. Two collaborators of prime importance were Alphonso Iannelli (1888-1965), artist and sculptor, and George M. Niedecken (1878-1945), interior designer. After Iannelli's spirited theater posters were brought to Wright's attention by his son John, Wright commissioned Iannelli to execute interior and exterior sculptural decoration for the important but ill-fated Midway Gardens. George Mann Niedecken of Milwaukee, Wisconsin, was an interior designer who not only executed many of Wright's early furniture designs, but helped coordinate the interior space for such landmark commissions as the Coonley and Robie residences. In addition to his collaboration with Frank Lloyd Wright, Niedecken also worked with several other Prairie architects, including Purcell and Elmslie, Percy D. Bentley, Elmer Grey, Spencer and Powers, Tallmadge and Watson, and William Drummond.

This growth period, which extended into the 1920s, has been labeled historically as the Prairie school. However, the philosophy of total design developed by these men is still being practiced today with the same degree of vigor and vitality that was germinated in the work of Furness, Richardson, Sullivan, and Wright. What has changed are the materials and the technologies available. While much of our contact with architectural design today is saturated with fast-food franchise buildings, gas station porcelain, modular metal buildings, and homes designed for magazines, there are still a number of architects who have maintained a relationship to the ideals of Frank Lloyd Wright's architecture and philosophy. These ideals are represented in the architecture of such men as Lloyd Wright, Taliesin Associated Architects, Bruce Goff, Arthur Carrara, William Wenzler, Herb Greene, among others.

The designs of Frank Lloyd Wright's son, Lloyd Wright (1890-1978), are both a continuation of and a departure from the style of his father. While deeply interested in town planning and landscape architecture, Lloyd Wright's architectural designs tend to reflect the climate and cultural values of Southern California. The firm of William Wenzler and Associates exhibits a strong sensitivity to natural materials, while at the same time grasping the premise of modular design technology. The buildings of Arthur Carrara provide the excitement of living and working spaces which contribute to a spirit of self-fulfillment and expression. And, of course, many of the later buildings of Frank Lloyd Wright's long and prolific career are still considered to represent America's most progressive examples of design.

Taliesin Associated Architects of the Frank Lloyd Wright Foundation have continued the philosophy of Wright in projects ranging from a summer retreat cottage to an environmental impact study of our transportation systems—always with a respect for material, setting, and humanity. John Howe, Herb Greene, Michael Johnson, and William Bruder continue to develop honest, organic approaches to the choices we can make in our homes, churches, schools, and places of work. And the architecture of Bruce Goff, using uncommon materials and forms, suggests an inventiveness which may well serve as an impetus for future approaches to design.

*The Prairie School Tradition* is comprised of selected

works documenting the Milwaukee exhibition. Although we feel we have scarcely scratched the surface of an exciting and vital architectural heritage, selections encompass the work of well-known and not-so-well-known architects and designers representing the totality of the design process. The exhibition was developed to reawaken our senses to indigenous, innovative American design, and the book is a permanent record of this wealth and heritage. Like the exhibition, the book neither expounds upon the architects or their architecture, nor does it attempt to interpret the design growth that has taken place. It is a presentation through fact and photograph. *The Prairie School Tradition* serves as a catalyst to remind us that individuality and freedom of expression is the basis of the American democratic system.

Brian A. Spencer, Architect
T. Victoria Hansen

# FRANK FURNESS (1839-1912)

Frank Furness was born in Philadelphia, Pennsylvania, and received his architectural training in the New York office of Richard Morris Hunt. It was in this stimulating environment that Furness was exposed to Viollet-le-Duc's theoretical concern for structure, John Ruskin's notion that nature must be the source for ornament, Owen Jones's proposition that "ornament should be based upon geometrical construction," as well as Hunt's Beaux Arts ideas of form and symbol in architecture. The modern principle of "form follows function" may have been transmitted to him through the early 19th-century architectural theory of the American sculptor Horatio Greenough and through contact with Ralph Waldo Emerson through Furness's father, the Reverend William Henry Furness. The relationship of Furness to the Prairie school is through Louis H. Sullivan, who was influenced by Furness while he was a draftsman in Furness's firm in 1873.

Frank Furness died relatively unknown in 1912. His forty-five active years of innovative contributions to Philadelphia architecture and his important role in the development of new American forms that evolved into the Prairie expression have only recently been appreciated.

Thomas Hockley Residence
Philadelphia, Pennsylvania    1875
Entrance porch and chimney detail
Photograph courtesy Cervin Robinson

Graver's Line Station
Philadelphia, Pennsylvania    Before 1884
Philadelphia and Reading Railroad Depot
(view from northwest)
Photograph courtesy Cervin Robinson

13

14     "Hedgely," William Windsor Residence
Ardmore, Pennsylvania    1887
Main stairhall, detail of fireback
Photograph courtesy Cervin Robinson

Williamson Free School of Mechanical Trades
Elwyn, Pennsylvania    1889
Main building from south
Photograph courtesy Cervin Robinson

Chapel, Mount Sinai Cemetery
Philadelphia, Pennsylvania 1891
Photograph courtesy Cervin Robinson

# HENRY HOBSON RICHARDSON (1838-1886)

Born and raised in Louisiana, Henry Hobson Richardson graduated from Harvard in 1859 and also studied at the École des Beaux Arts in Paris. He returned to the United States and in 1866 began a practice which remained based in the East, although fame and success brought him commissions throughout the country, most notably in Chicago. Richardson served as a transitional figure between the styles and principles of the past and the birth of a truly "modern" architecture. More than any other architect, Richardson was to change the architect's role as a designer of homes and commercial buildings for the wealthy to a much broader activity encompassing a wide range of building types. Richardson's architecture is noted above all for its dynamic use of forms and materials and for its interest in the correspondence between the building's interior and exterior and its overall relationship to the environment. His spatial innovations, as well as his advocation of the use of natural, unfinished materials would become basic characteristics of the Prairie style. Richardson's ornament, which displayed a shift away from stylized, historical forms to more imaginative patterns, would also have a profound effect on the Chicago architects, especially on the style of Louis H. Sullivan.

Gate Lodge
North Easton, Massachusetts    1880-1881
Photograph circa 1880s
Photograph courtesy Houghton Library,
Harvard College

18    Crane Memorial Library
      Quincy, Massachusetts    1880-1882
      Photograph circa 1880s
      Photograph courtesy Houghton Library,
      Harvard College

Bridges, Back Bay Fens
Boston, Massachusetts    1880-1884
Photograph by Jean Baer O'Gorman,
Courtesy Houghton Library,
Harvard College

20   Marshall Field Wholesale Store
     Chicago, Illinois    1885-1887
     Photograph taken after 1900
     Photograph courtesy David R. Phillips Studio

J. J. Glessner Residence
Chicago, Illinois    1886
Pencil on tracing paper
6¾ × 15½″ (17 × 39 cm)
Photograph courtesy Houghton Library,
Harvard College

# ADLER & SULLIVAN (1880-1895)

## DANKMAR ADLER (1844-1900)
## LOUIS H. SULLIVAN (1856-1924)

Dankmar Adler was born in Lengsfeld, Germany, in 1844 and immigrated to the United States with his parents at the age of ten. His first apprenticeship, after cutting short his education, was with E. Willart Smith, a Detroit architect. Although his career was interrupted by the Civil War, he resumed it after 1866 in Chicago, first in association with the office of O. S. Kinney, then in partnership with Kinney's son, and, later in the partnership of Burling and Adler, which was eventually replaced by D. Adler & Co. in 1878.

Louis Henri Sullivan, born in 1856 in Boston, began his career after only one year of study at the Massachusetts Institute of Technology. He left with the intent of studying at the École des Beaux-Arts in Paris, but was unable to because he was too young. Instead Sullivan began an apprenticeship in the Philadelphia firm of Furness & Hewitt, which lasted until he had a confrontation with George Hewitt. That and the depression of 1873 and resultant decline of construction in Philadelphia, prodded Sullivan to venture to Chicago, a city rebuilding after the great fire of 1871. Sullivan selected his next employer by walking the streets and tracking down the name of the architect of a building he admired. This led him to William LeBaron Jenney, architect of the Portland Block. In 1874, Sullivan enrolled in the École des Beaux-Arts, but, feeling the school had little to offer, returned to Chicago in 1875 and became a draftsman in the firm of Johnston and Edelman.

Sullivan began work with D. Adler & Co. in 1879, becoming a partner in 1880 and receiving equal status with Dankmar Adler in 1881. This partnership was to last until 1895. During this time the firm of Adler & Sullivan executed a number of notable buildings, including the Auditorium Building in Chicago of 1887-1889, the Chicago Stock Exchange Building of 1893-1894, the Guaranty Building in Buffalo of 1894-1895, the Schiller Building in Chicago of 1891-1892, the Transportation Building at the 1893 World Colombian Exposition in Chicago, and the Wainwright Building of 1890-1891 in St. Louis.

Adler left the partnership in 1895 for a short-lived position as consulting architect and general sales manager with the Crane Elevator Company. Adler and Sullivan were unable to rectify their break in partnership because Sullivan felt Adler had deserted him, although the firm had had no work, and they each formed independent practices. Adler died shortly thereafter in 1900 and Sullivan's practice dwindled in size after the completion in 1899 of the Carson, Pirie, Scott store (then called Schlesinger and Mayer).

Sullivan's practice after 1900 consisted mainly of small Midwestern banks and commercial buildings. The high point was the masterpiece National Farmers' Bank at Owatonna, Minnesota, and the low ebb two years before his death, the design of the facade for the Krause Music Store for architect William Presto.

Beyond the completion of architectural designs, Adler's contributions in acoustics and theater design are significant and Sullivan's writings in *Kindergarten Chats and Other Writings* and his description of delineation in a series of plates, *A System of Ornament,* are constant sources of study. As well as producing great architectural achievement, Adler & Sullivan provided the seeds for growth of contemporary American architecture.

D. Adler & Co. (1878-1880)
M. Wineman, Esq., Residence
Chicago, Illinois     1882
Column capital, pencil on paper
Delineated by Louis H. Sullivan
24⅞ × 28⅛″ (63 × 73 cm)
Courtesy Avery Library, Columbia University

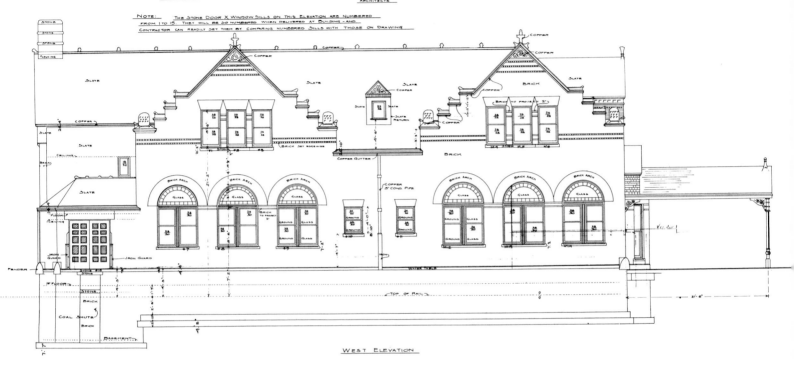

WEST ELEVATION

**24** Oakland Passenger House for the Illinois
Central Railroad
Chicago, Illinois    1886
Ink on linen
18¾ × 35⅜'' (48 × 90 cm)
Courtesy Thomas A. Heinz, Architect

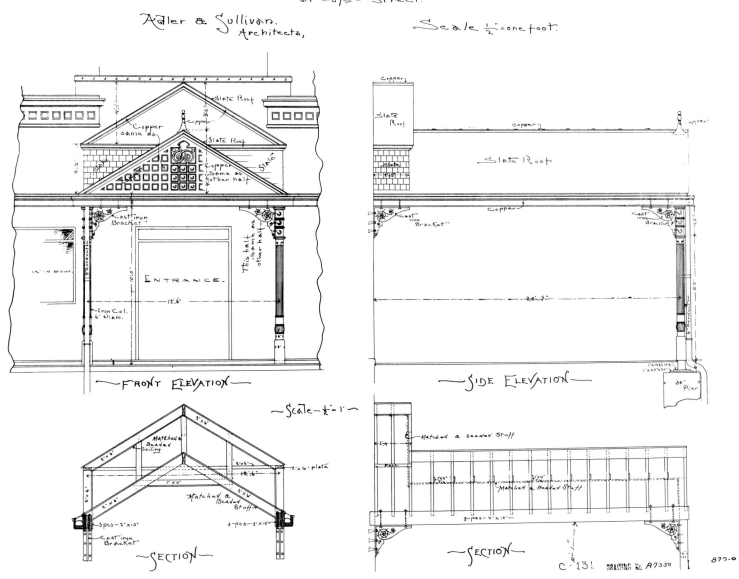

Veranda Roof over Walk and South Entrance
of The Illinois Central Passenger Station
at —39th— Street.

Adler & Sullivan.
Architects,

Scale ½"=one foot.

— FRONT ELEVATION —

— SIDE ELEVATION —

~Scale-½"=1'~

—SECTION—

—SECTION—

Oakland Passenger House for the Illinois
Central Railroad
Chicago, Illinois    1886
Ink on linen
21⅛ × 26⅛" (54 × 66 cm)
Courtesy Thomas A. Heinz, Architect

25

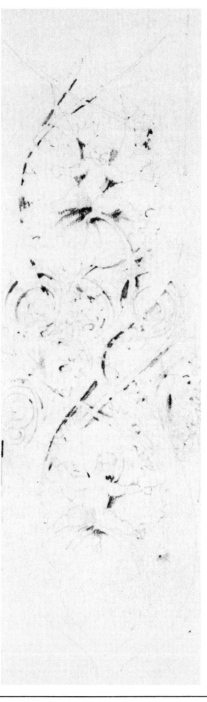

**26**    Schiller Building
Chicago, Illinois    1891-1892
Ornamental detail, plaster
7¾ × 14″ (20 × 36 cm)
Courtesy Mr. & Mrs. Irving D. Saltstein

Transportation Building, World's Columbian
Exposition
Chicago, Illinois    1892-1893
Ornamental door jamb, pencil on paper
6⅞ × 4¼″ (17 × 11 cm)
Courtesy Avery Library, Columbia University

Transportation Building
World's Columbian Exposition
Chicago, Illinois    1892-1893
Photograph from Morrison, *Louis Sullivan:*
*The Prophet of Modern Architecture*

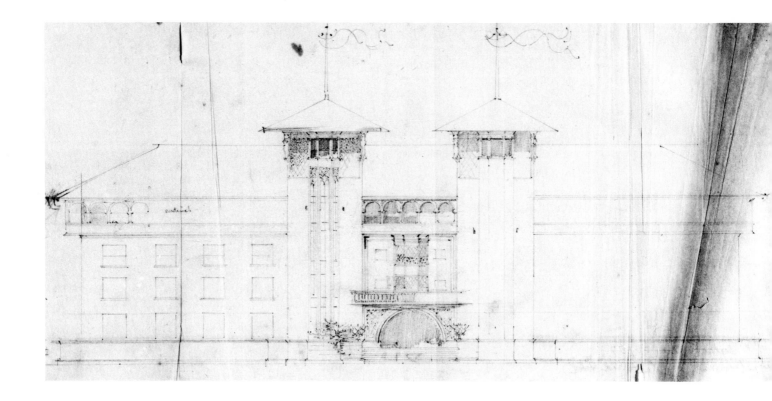

28    Victoria Hotel
      Chicago Heights, Illinois    1892-1893
      Pencil on tracing paper
      8¾ × 17½" (22 × 44 cm)
      Courtesy The Burnham Library, The Art
      Institute of Chicago

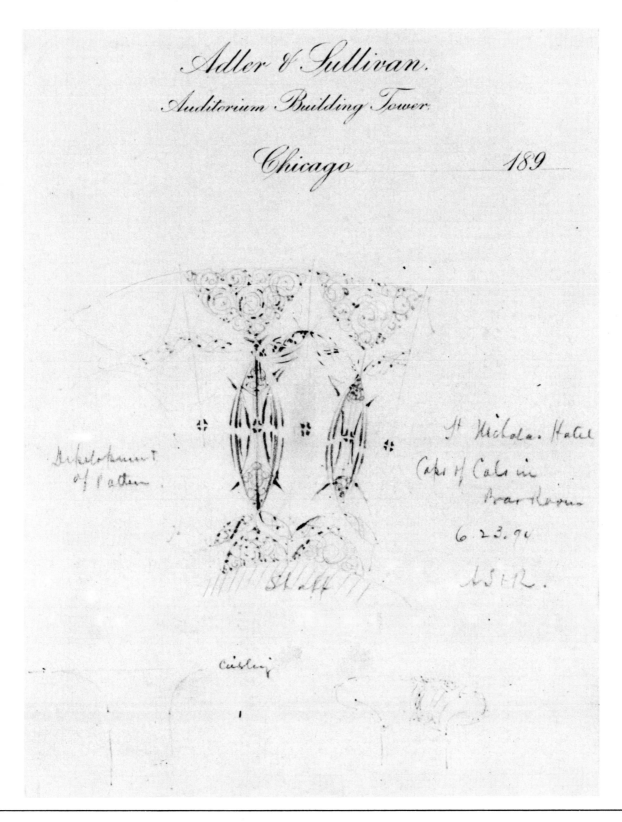

St. Nicholas Hotel
St. Louis, Missouri     1894
Caps of columns in bar room,
pencil on paper
8¼ × 5¼" (21 × 14 cm)
Courtesy Avery Library, Columbia University

30

Wainwright Building
St. Louis, Missouri    1891
Door knob and escutcheon, cast iron
11¼ × 2¼ × 2½" (29 × 6 × 6 cm)
Courtesy Mr. & Mrs. Irving D. Saltstein

Guaranty Building
Buffalo, New York    1894-1895
Door knob and escutcheon, bronze
Courtesy United Founders Life Insurance
Company of Illinois and Louis Sullivan
Architecture Museum

Chicago Stock Exchange Building
Chicago, Illinois     1894
Stairway balusters, bronze
Courtesy Earl Talbot and George Talbot

32    Chicago Stock Exchange Building
      Chicago, Illinois    1894
      Elevator grilles, wrought metal
      74 × 29½" (188 × 75 cm)
      Courtesy Northwestern University,
      Evanston, Illinois

      Guaranty Building
      Buffalo, New York    1894-1895
      Column capital fragments, terra cotta
      12 × 18 × 19" (31 × 46 × 48 cm)
      (two pieces)
      Courtesy United Founders Life Insurance
      Company of Illinois and Louis Sullivan
      Architecture Museum

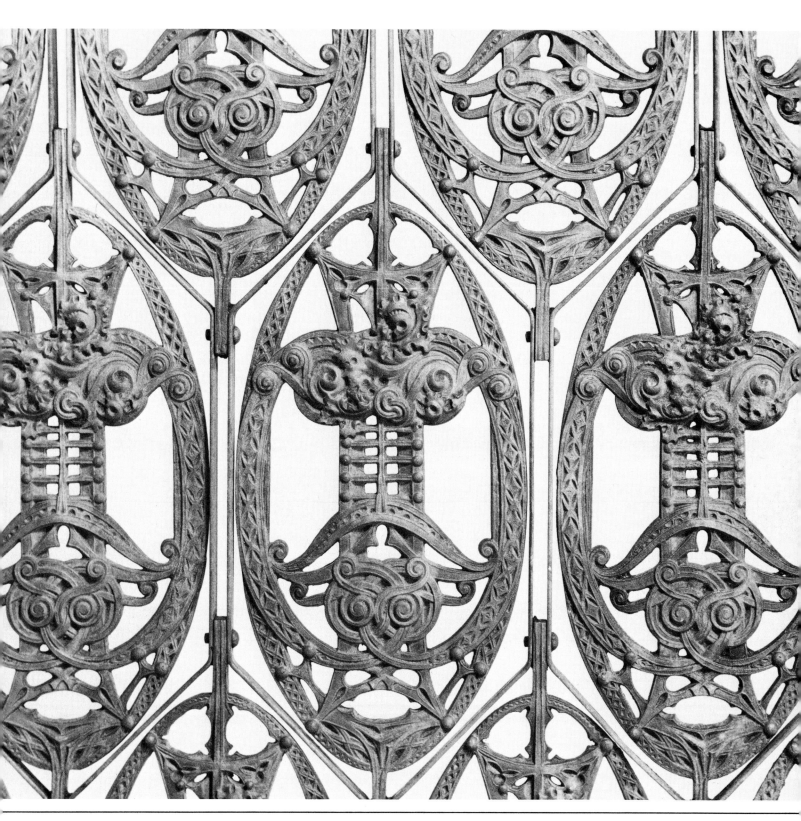

Guaranty Building
Buffalo, New York    1894-1895
Detail, elevator grille, bronze-coated cast iron
Courtesy United Founders Life Insurance
Company of Illinois and Louis Sullivan
Architecture Museum

**34** Guaranty Building
Buffalo, New York    1894-1895
Detail, elevator base, bronze-coated cast iron
7 × 86″ (18 × 218 cm)
Courtesy United Founders Life Insurance
Company of Illinois and Louis Sullivan
Architecture Museum

Guaranty Building
Buffalo, New York    1894-1895
Stairway baluster, bronze-coated cast iron
31 × 10″ (79 × 25 cm)
Courtesy United Founders Life Insurance
Company of Illinois and Louis Sullivan
Architecture Museum

Carson, Pirie, Scott & Co. (originally the
Schlesinger & Mayer Department Store)
Chicago, Illinois    1899-1904
Stairway baluster, cast iron
34⅞ × 9¾″ (89 × 25 cm)
Gift of Carson, Pirie, Scott & Co. through
The Art Institute of Chicago

35

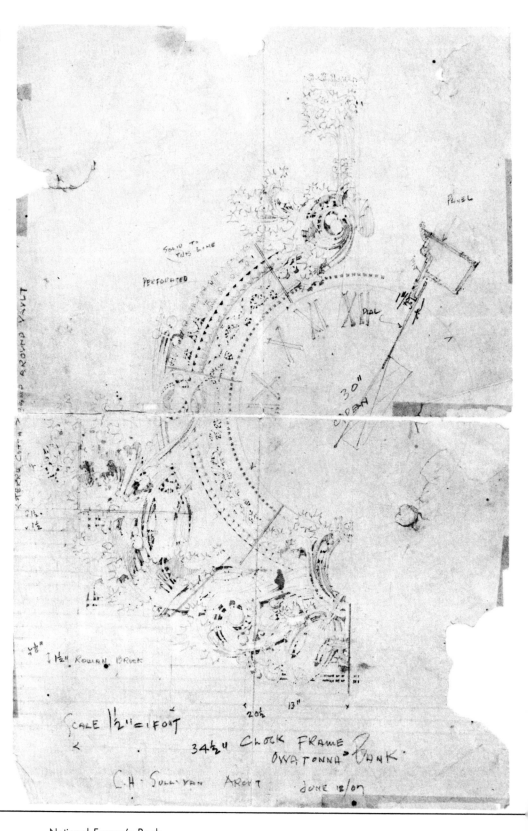

National Farmer's Bank
Owatonna, Minnesota    1907
Ornamental clock frame, pencil on paper
11⅞ × 7⅞″ (30 × 20 cm)
Courtesy Avery Library, Columbia University

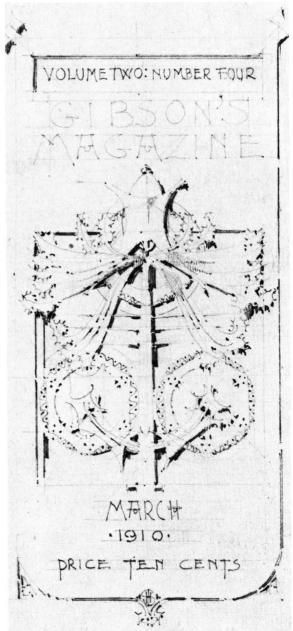

National Farmer's Bank
Owatonna, Minnesota    1907
Teller's wicket, copper-plated cast iron
41 × 22¾" (104 × 58 cm)
Courtesy The Art Institute of Chicago

Cover design for *Gibson's* Magazine
(Volume 2, Number 4, March 1910)
Pencil on paper
8½ × 4⅛" (22 × 10 cm)
Courtesy Avery Library, Columbia University

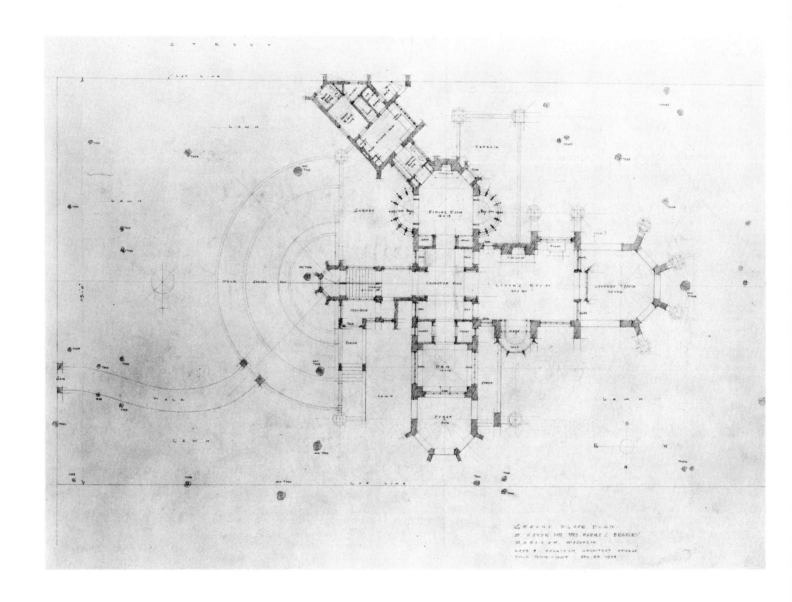

**38**   Harold C. Bradley Residence
Madison, Wisconsin    1908-1910
Ground floor plan, scheme 1, 1908,
pencil on paper
33¼ × 35¾″ (85 × 91 cm)
Courtesy Northwest Architectural Archives,
University of Minnesota

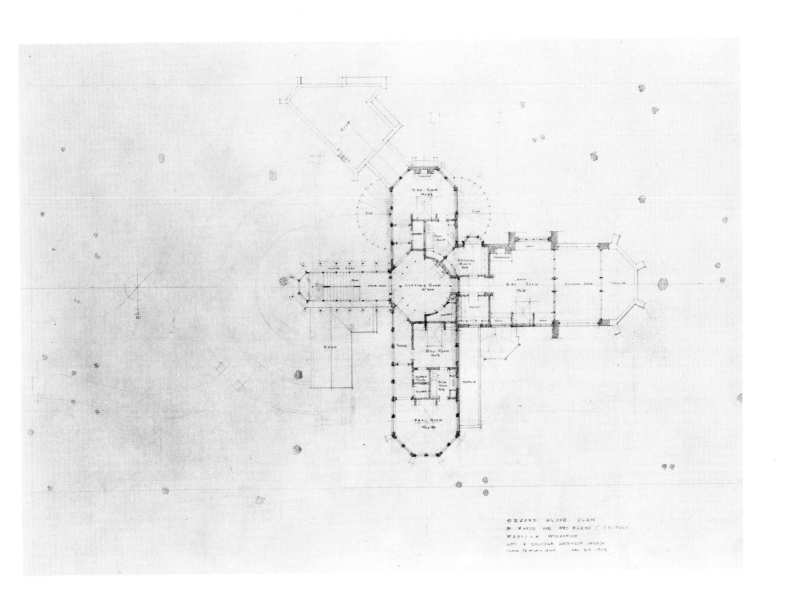

Harold C. Bradley Residence
Madison, Wisconsin     1908-1910
Second floor plan, scheme 1, 1908,
pencil on paper
33¼ × 35¾" (85 × 91 cm)
Courtesy Northwest Architectural Archives,
University of Minnesota

**40**  Harold C. Bradley Residence
Madison, Wisconsin    1908-1910
East elevation, scheme 1, 1908,
pencil on paper
32½ × 25½" (83 × 65 cm)
Courtesy Northwest Architectural Archives,
University of Minnesota

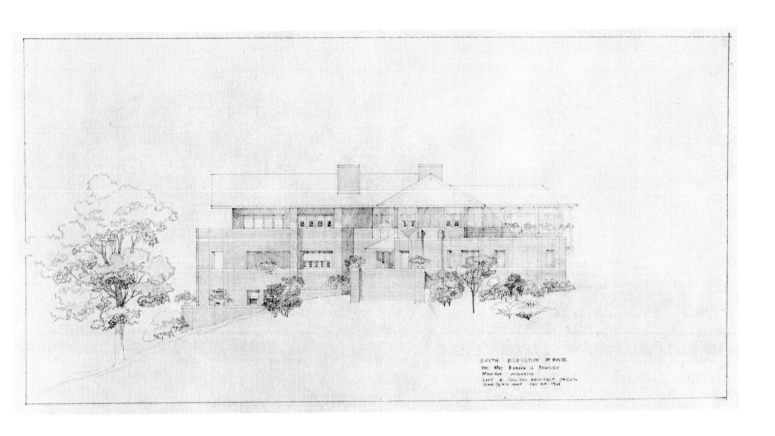

Harold C. Bradley Residence
Madison, Wisconsin    1908-1910
South elevation, scheme 1, 1908,
pencil on paper
32½ × 25½″ (83 × 65 cm)
Courtesy Northwest Architectural Archives,
University of Minnesota

42                         Harold C. Bradley Residence
Madison, Wisconsin     1908-1910
Side chair for dining room, oak with
upholstered seat
49½ × 20 × 20⅜" (126 × 51 × 52 cm)
Courtesy Alpha of Wisconsin Sigma Phi

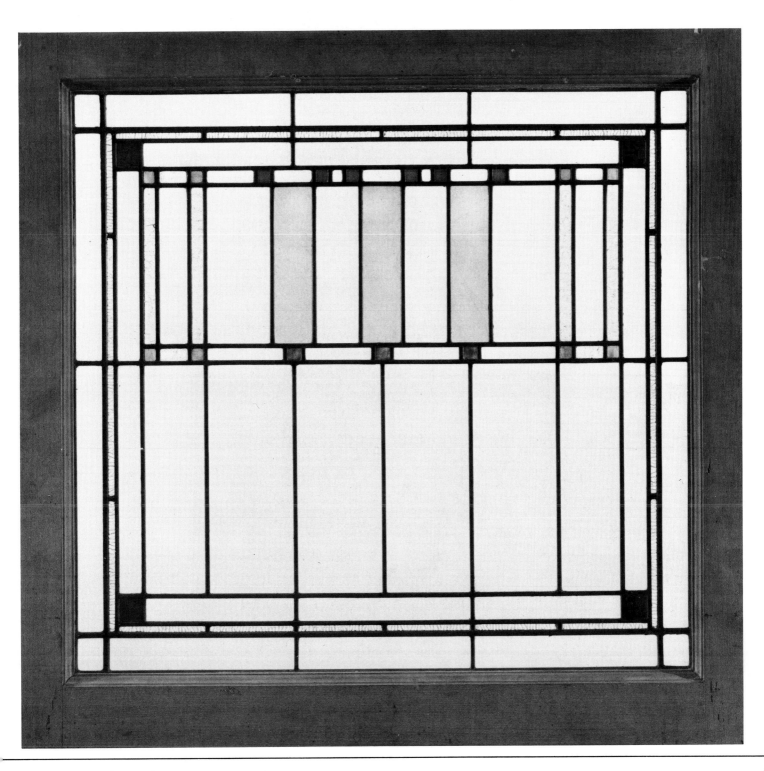

Harold C. Bradley Residence
Madison, Wisconsin      1908-1910
Windows (2), art glass
33¼ × 35⅞″ (85 × 91 cm) and
32½ × 25¾″ (83 × 66 cm)
Courtesy Alpha of Wisconsin Sigma Phi

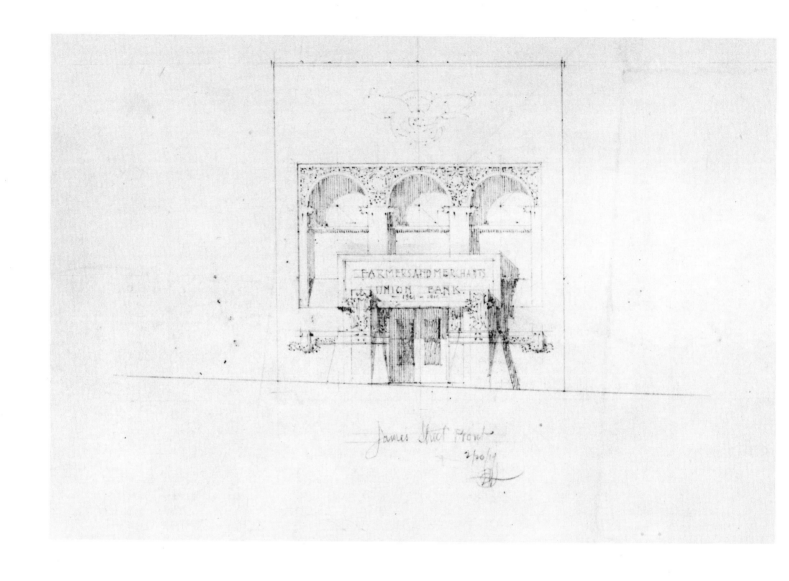

**44** Farmers' and Merchants' Union Bank
Columbus, Wisconsin    1919
James Street front,
pencil on paper
15 × 20″ (38 × 51 cm)
Courtesy The Burnham Library, The Art
Institute of Chicago

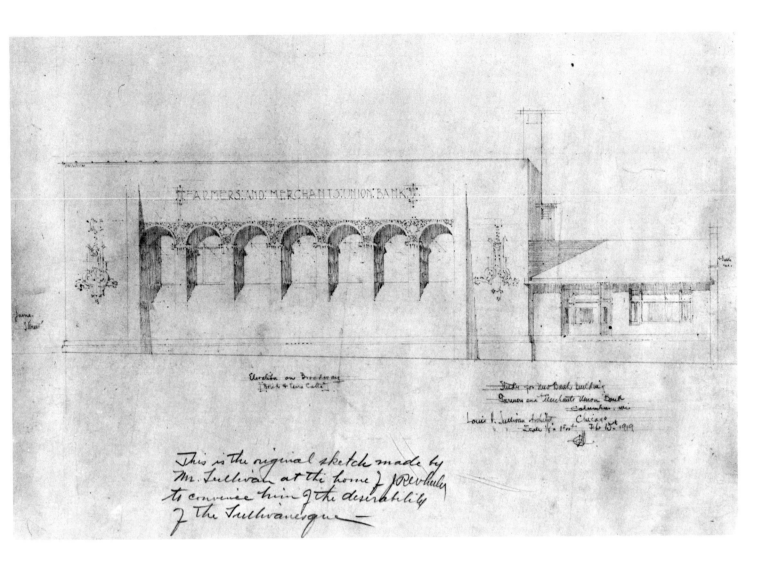

Farmers' and Merchants' Union Bank
Columbus, Wisconsin    1919
Elevation on Broadway, pencil on paper
15 × 20" (38 × 51 cm)
Courtesy The Burnham Library, The Art
Institute of Chicago

# FRANK LLOYD WRIGHT (1867-1959)

Frank Lloyd Wright was born in Richland Center, Wisconsin. Wright's architectural education consisted of one year as a special student in the engineering curriculum at the University of Wisconsin. His apprenticeship training began with a brief stay in the office of Alan D. Conover, dean of the Engineering Department. In 1887, Wright left Madison for Chicago where he was employed in the office of Joseph Lyman Silsbee. This too was a brief stay and in less than six months he began work in the office of Adler & Sullivan. In 1893, after dispute over his independent work, Wright left his position as chief draftsman to begin independent practice—a practice that was to have an unprecedented effect on American architecture.

The William Winslow Residence of 1893 was the first of over 700 designs he was to produce in over seventy years of architectural practice. Working in the early years from his Oak Park home and studio, Wright generated a new sense of architectural form and space in America in the evolution of the Prairie house. He likened its physical design elements—low proportions to enhance the round lines of the Midwest prairies, horizontal bands of windows to work with the changing seasons, hovering roofs to protect the buildings, and an openness of plan—to the Oriental philosophy expressed in *The Book of Tea*. "The reality of a room was to be found in the space enclosed by the roof and walls, not in the roof and walls themselves." Obviously this thought stayed with him, as the Prairie houses are each a study in the flow of space, from the intimacy of the entry to the open excitement of the main rooms.

Wright's home and studio was not just a place of living and working; it was an experimental study, constantly being remodeled and revised, which also served as a source of new ideas. The playroom addition of 1895, for example, becomes the ballroom design of the Susan Lawrence Dana Residence of 1901-1902.

Often new building designs were inspired by earlier projects. Wright noted that the Yahara Boat Club of 1902 was related to Unity Temple of 1906. Roof forms of the Chauncey Williams Residence of 1895 reappear in the designs for the Lake Tahoe cottages of 1924. Certainly Midway Gardens of 1912 is the model for the Imperial Hotel of 1915-1916, and the Coonley Playhouse windows of 1911 suggest the integration of forms that emerged in Usonian house concepts.

Not only did Wright develop new design forms, but he instituted such technological changes as indirect lighting, casement windows, and what are today called passive environmental controls, as well as radiant floor heating, first used in the Herbert Jacobs Residence in 1936. When architectural commissions were scarce, Wright produced a profuse amount of written material that firmly established his philosophy.

As many architects and designers returned in the mid-1930s to more traditional building forms, Wright introduced new dimensions in design thought in America with the 1935 Edgar J. Kaufmann Residence, "Falling Water," the Jacobs Residence of 1936 (the beginning of the Usonian house concept), the S.C. Johnson Administration Building of 1936, and concepts for decentralized living, which he called Broadacre City. To extend his philosophy beyond his buildings and writings, he and Olgivanna Wright founded the Taliesin Fellowship in 1932. This brought a new generation of students who apprenticed by working in the drafting room and constructing the buildings they drew, as well as participating in theater, dance, music, and art.

The highlights of Frank Lloyd Wright's work shown here support his position as the master of American architecture. Wright offered a contemporary architecture, fitted to the social, cultural, and technological changes of a modern society. Today his name is synonymous with American architectural design, even to the layperson with little knowledge of the profession.

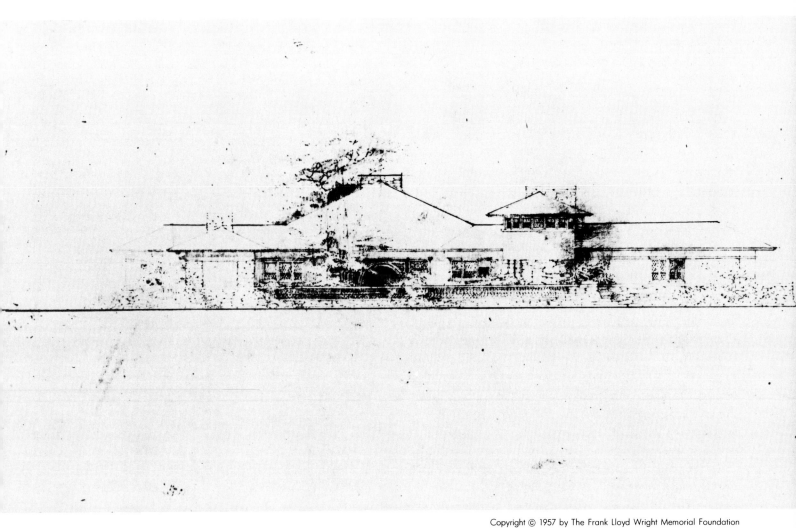

Drawing shown to Louis Sullivan when
applying for a job      1887
Courtesy The Frank Lloyd Wright
Memorial Foundation

48     Robert Roloson Apartments
Chicago, Illinois    1894
Ornamental baluster, terra cotta
16⅞ × 7⅞ × 7⅞" (43 × 20 × 20 cm)
Courtesy Marilyn and Wilbert Hasbrouck

Glass designs for American Luxfer
Prism Company
Chicago, Illinois    1895
Glass prisms set into metal frame
24⅝ × 27⅞ (63 × 71 cm)
Courtesy Robert Uchner Studio

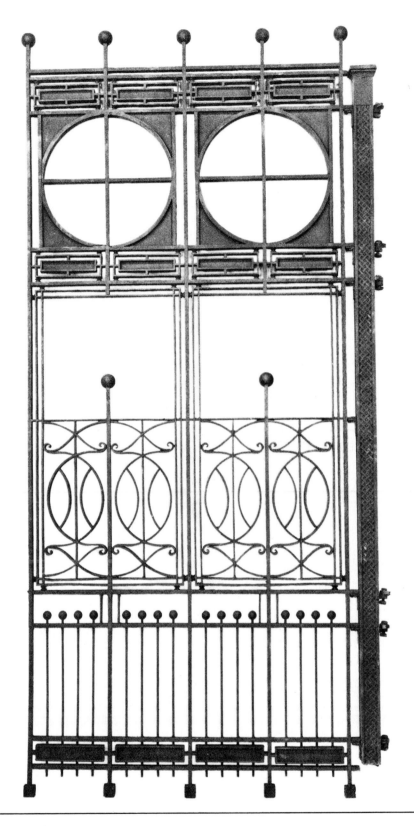

Francis Apartments
Chicago, Illinois     1895
Entrance gate, wrought iron
98 × 49½″ (249 × 126 cm)
Courtesy The Art Institute of Chicago, Gift
of the Graham Foundation for Advanced
Studies in the Fine Arts

50    Charles E. Roberts Residence
      Oak Park, Illinois    1895-1896
      Pedestal library table, oak
      30½ × 47″ (78 × 119 cm)
      Courtesy The Art Institute of Chicago, Gift
      of Mr. Roger White in memory of
      Charles E. Roberts

Flower studies    1897
Ink on paper
4¾ × 3″ (12 × 8 cm) and
5 × 2½″ (13 × 6 cm)
Courtesy Walter W. Schmidt

Vase    1893-1902
Copper
28 × 4½ × 4½″
(71 × 11 × 11 cm)
Courtesy Edgar Kaufmann, Jr.

52    Arm chair    circa 1902
Attributed to Frank Lloyd Wright
Oak with upholstered cushions
33 × 37 × 28 (84 × 94 × 71 cm)
Courtesy The Frank Lloyd Wright Home and
Studio Foundation

Dana Residence
Springfield, Illinois     1903
Dining room scheme, pencil, pastels, and
washes on brown paper
Courtesy Avery Library, Columbia University

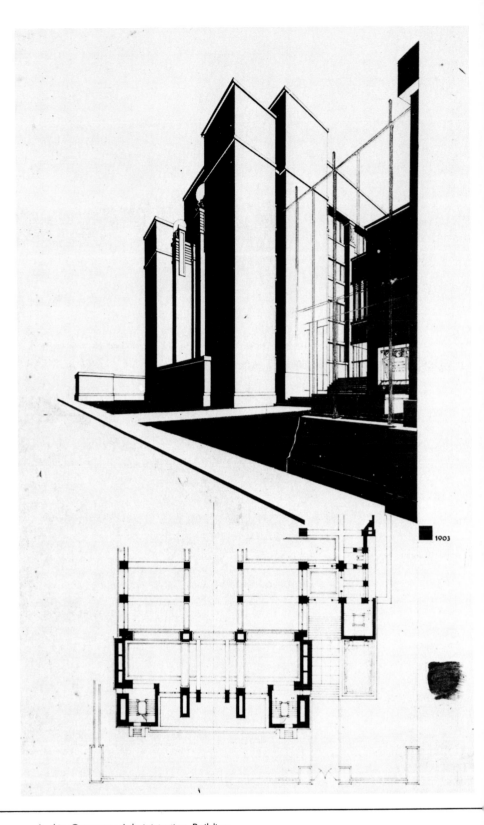

1903

Larkin Company Administration Building
Buffalo, New York    1903
Courtesy The Frank Lloyd Wright
Memorial Foundation

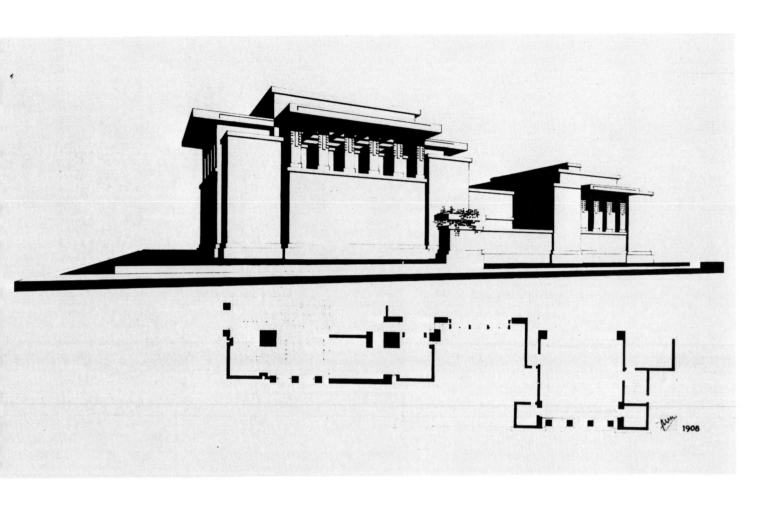

Unity Temple
Oak Park, Illinois     1904
Courtesy The Frank Lloyd Wright
Memorial Foundation

56    Unity Temple
      Oak Park, Illinois    1903
      Photograph courtesy Thomas A. Heinz,
      Architect
      © Copyright Thomas A. Heinz 1979

Unity Temple
Oak Park, Illinois    1904
Side chair, oak with upholstered seat
39⅜ × 15 × 18⅝" (100 × 38 × 47 cm)
Courtesy The Third Unitarian Church,
Oak Park, Illinois

58    Darwin D. Martin Residence
      Buffalo, New York    1904
      "Tree of Life" abstraction, art glass
      41½ × 26¼" (105 × 67 cm)
      Courtesy The Art Institute of Chicago, Gift
      of the Antiquarian Society,
      Mrs. Phillip K. Wrigley Fund

      Darwin D. Martin Residence
      Buffalo, New York    1904
      Fireplace study, pencil and watercolor on
      tracing paper
      Delineated by George M. Niedecken
      9 × 12" (23 × 31 cm)
      Courtesy Mr. & Mrs. Robert L. Jacobson

Darwin D. Martin Residence
Buffalo, New York     1904
Arm chair, oak with upholstered seat
31½ × 22 × 22¼" (80 × 56 × 56 cm)
Courtesy The State University of New York
at Buffalo

59

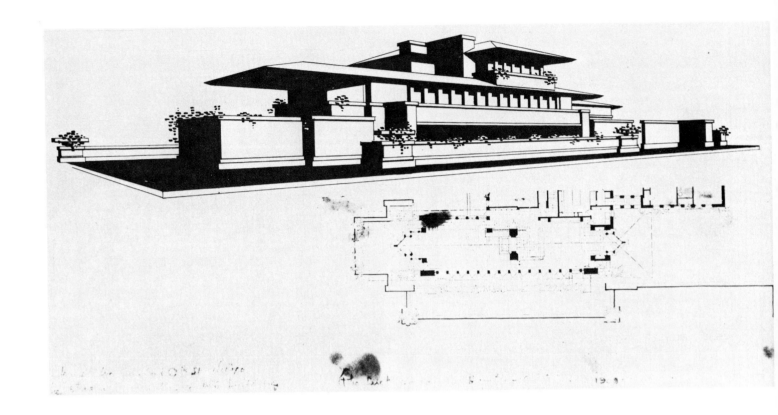

60    Frederick C. Robie Residence
Chicago, Illinois    1906
Courtesy The Frank Lloyd Wright
Memorial Foundation

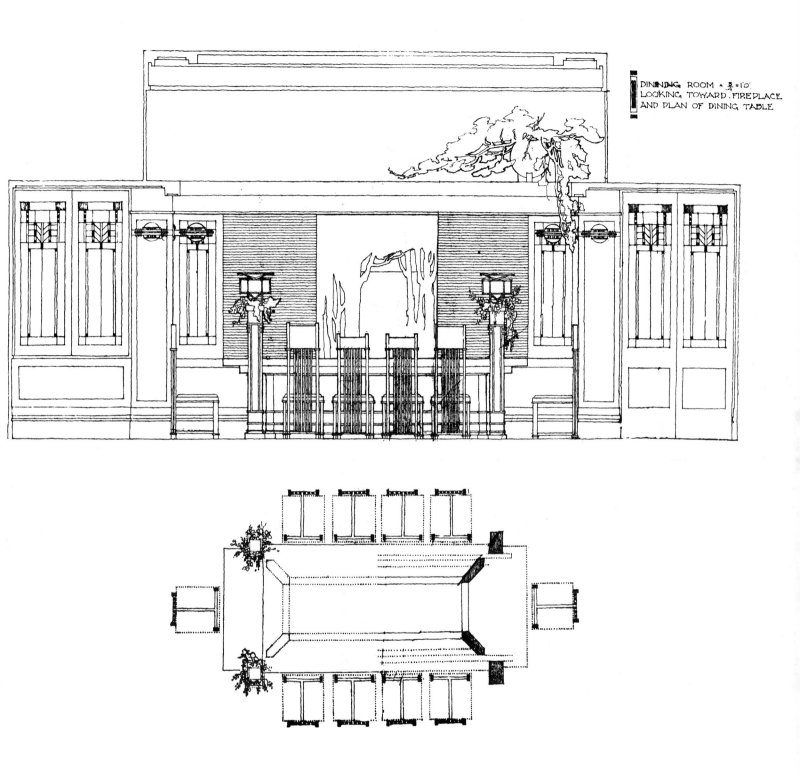

DINING ROOM ⅜"=1'0"
LOOKING TOWARD FIREPLACE
AND PLAN OF DINING TABLE

Possibly Frederick C. Robie Residence
Chicago, Illinois    1906
Dining room scheme, brown ink on paper
Delineation attributed to Marion Mahoney
23 × 25½" (58 × 65 cm)
Courtesy Mr. & Mrs. Robert L. Jacobson

61

62    Frederick C. Robie Residence
Chicago, Illinois    1906
Dining room
Photograph courtesy Mr. & Mrs. Robert L.
Jacobson

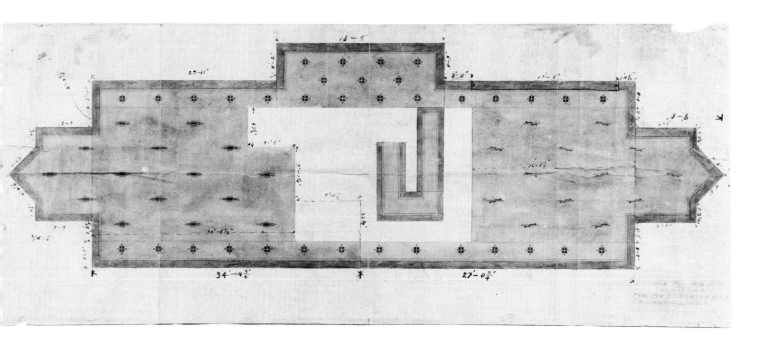

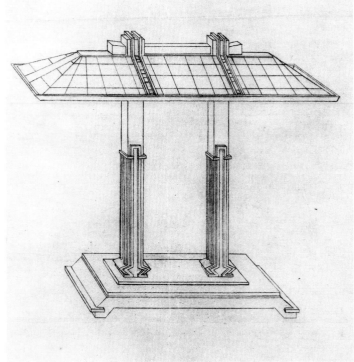

Top
Frederick C. Robie Residence
Chicago, Illinois    1906
Living, dining, and hall rug layout,
watercolor on kraft paper
15¾ × 40½" (40 × 103 cm)
Courtesy Mr. & Mrs. Robert L. Jacobson

Bottom left
Frederick C. Robie Residence
Chicago, Illinois    1906
Breakfast table, pencil on kraft paper
6½ × 8" (17 × 20 cm)
Courtesy Mr. & Mrs. Robert L. Jacobson

Bottom right
Frederick C. Robie Residence
Chicago, Illinois    1906
Living room lamp, pencil on tracing paper
Delineated by George M. Niedecken
11¾ × 9" ( 30 × 23 cm)
Courtesy Mr. & Mrs. Robert L. Jacobson

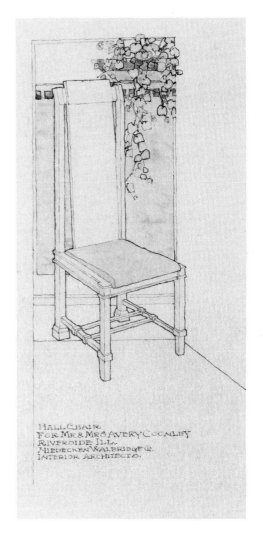

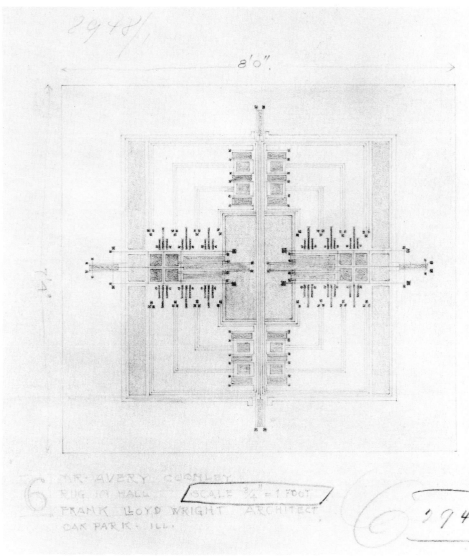

Avery Coonley Residence
Riverside, Illinois    1907
Hall chair, ink and watercolor on paper
Delineated by George M. Niedecken
9¾ × 6" (25 × 15 cm)
Courtesy Mr. & Mrs. Robert L. Jacobson

Avery Coonley Residence
Riverside, Illinois    1907
Design for rug in hall, colored pencil on
tracing paper
8¾ × 9⅛" (22 × 23 cm)
Courtesy Mr. & Mrs. Robert L. Jacobson

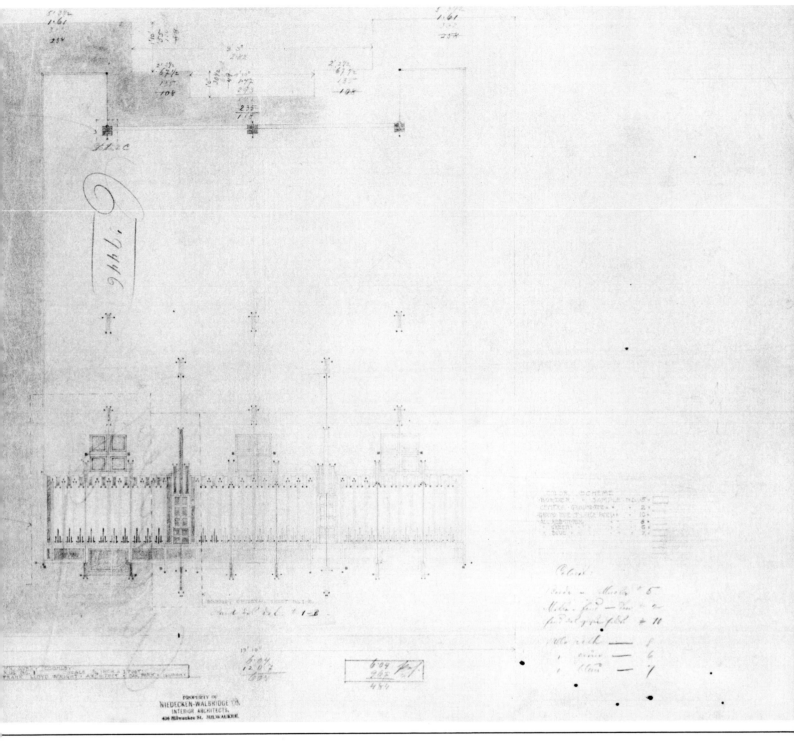

Avery Coonley Residence
Riverside, Illinois    1907
Design for rug no. 1, colored pencil on
tracing paper
21½ × 31¼″ (55 × 80 cm)
Courtesy Mr. & Mrs. Robert L. Jacobson

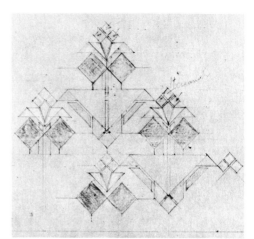

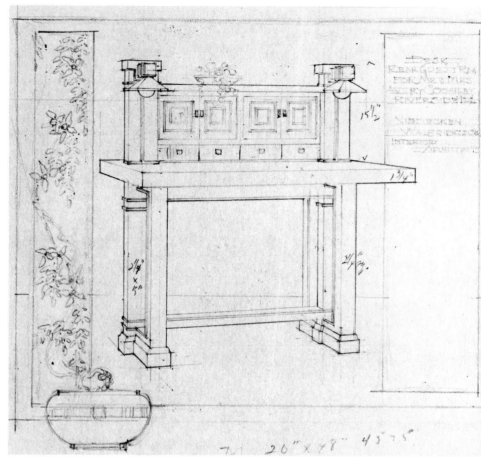

**66**  Avery Coonley Residence
Riverside, Illinois    1907
Tile design
Courtesy The Frank Lloyd Wright
Memorial Foundation

Avery Coonley Residence
Riverside, Illinois    1907
Desk for rear guest room, pencil on kraft paper
Delineated by George M. Niedecken
7½ × 5½" (19 × 14 cm)
Courtesy Mr. & Mrs. Robert L. Jacobson

Avery Coonley Residence (?)
Riverside, Illinois    1907
Desk, oak
44 × 42 × 25⅞" (112 × 107 × 66 cm)
Courtesy Dr. & Mrs. Jeffrey Kunz, courtesy
the Elvehjem Art Center

**68**  Isabel Roberts Residence
River Forest, Illinois    1908
Side chair
Courtesy Chicago School of Architecture
Foundation, Chicago, Illinois

Robert W. Evans Residence
Chicago, Illinois    1908
Armchair, oak with upholstered cushion
34½ × 30⅛ × 23⅞" (88 × 77 × 61 cm)
Courtesy The Art Institute of Chicago,
Gift of Mr. & Mrs. F. M. Fahrenwald

Robert W. Evans Residence
Chicago, Illinois    1908
Library table, oak
28¾ × 36 × 66" (73 × 91 × 168 cm)
Courtesy The Art Institute of Chicago,
Gift of Mr. & Mrs. F. M. Fahrenwald

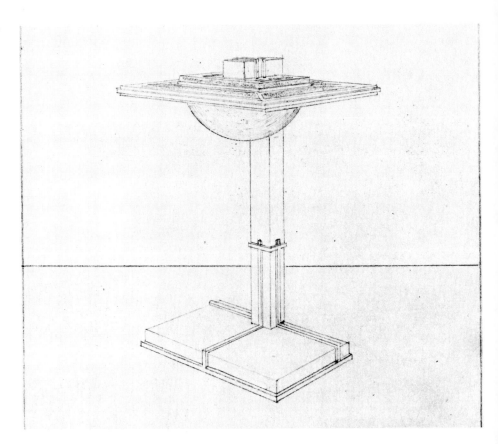

70

Meyer May Residence
Grand Rapids, Michigan    1908
Table lamp, pencil on tracing paper
Delineated by George M. Niedecken
8¼ × 5¾" (21 × 15 cm)
Courtesy Mr. & Mrs. Robert L. Jacobson

Meyer May Residence
Grand Rapids, Michigan    1908
Dining table and chairs,
pencil on tracing paper
Delineated by George M. Niedecken
6¾ × 9¾" (17 × 25 cm)
Courtesy Mr. & Mrs. Robert L. Jacobson

OAK PARK 1904

Mrs. Thomas Gale Residence
Oak Park, Illinois     1904-1909
Courtesy The Frank Lloyd Wright
Memorial Foundation

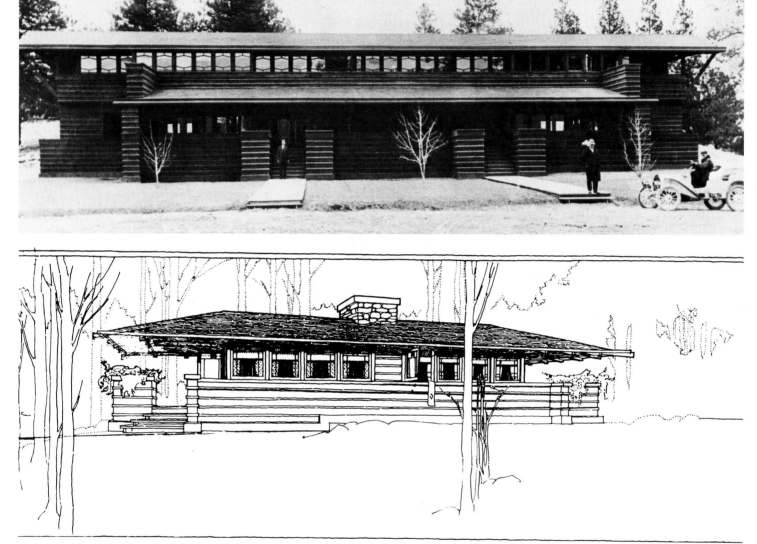

72   Bitter Root Inn
     Darby, Montana    1909
     Courtesy The Frank Lloyd Wright Memorial
     Foundation

     Como Orchard Land Company
     Bitter Root Valley, Darby, Montana
     Cabin
     Courtesy The Frank Lloyd Wright Memorial
     Foundation

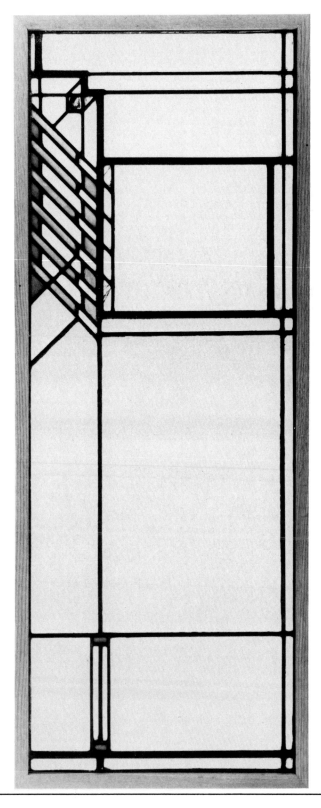

Oscar Steffens Residence
Chicago, Illinois    1909
Window, art glass
42½ × 16¼″ (108 × 41 cm)
Courtesy Mr. & Mrs. Timothy Samuelson

**74**    E. P. Irving Residence
Decatur, Illinois    1910
Rug designs, ink and watercolor on tracing paper
Delineated by George M. Niedecken
21 × 34¾″ (53 × 88 cm)
Courtesy Mr. & Mrs. Robert L. Jacobson

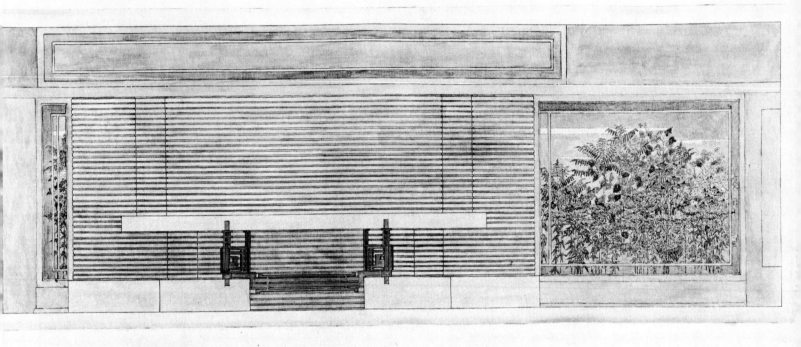

E. P. Irving Residence
Decatur, Illinois    1910
Living room fireplace and mural decoration,
ink and watercolor on cloth
Delineated by George M. Niedecken
28 × 26" (71 × 66 cm)
Courtesy Mr. & Mrs. Robert L. Jacobson

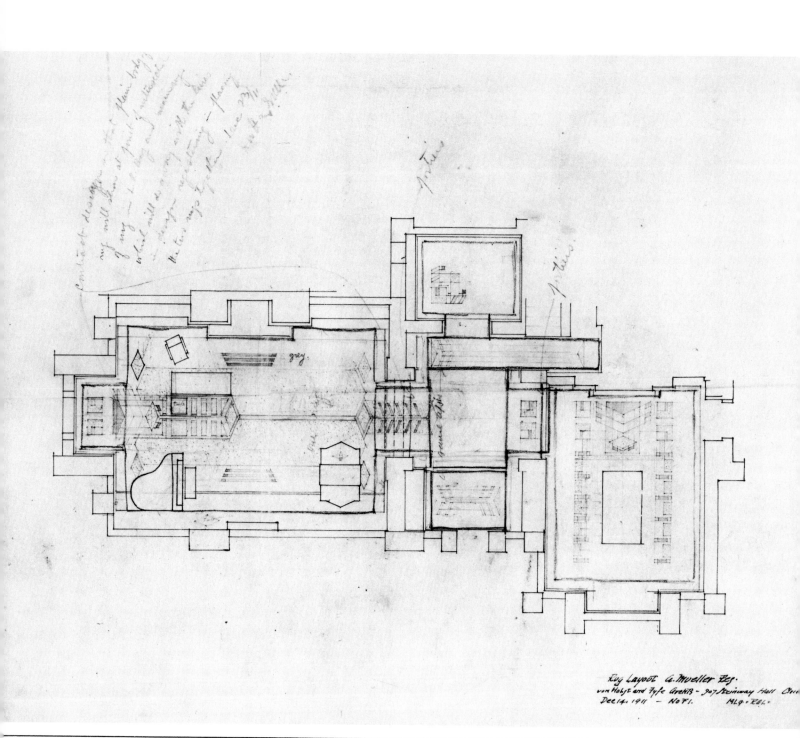

**76**  Adolph Mueller Residence
Decatur, Illinois    1911
Rug layout, pencil and ink on tracing paper
18 × 30″ (46 × 76 cm)
Courtesy Mr. & Mrs. Robert L. Jacobson

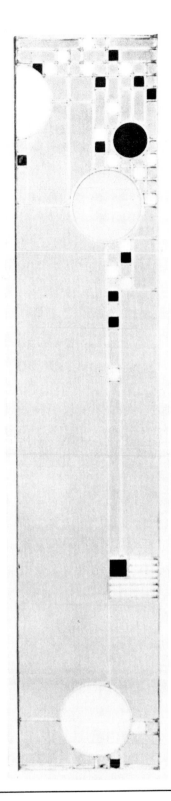

Avery Coonley Playhouse
Riverside, Illinois    1911-1912
Window, art glass
62 × 13⅝″ (158 × 35 cm)
Courtesy Dawn and Walter Netsch

Avery Coonley Playhouse
Riverside, Illinois    1911-1912
Adult side chair, wood with upholstery
37 × 15 × 18½″ (94 × 38 × 47 cm)
Courtesy Marilyn and Wilbert Hasbrouck

78    Lake Geneva Hotel
      (For Arthur L. Richards Company)
      Lake Geneva, Wisconsin    1911
      Tempera on illustration board
      13⅞ × 51½" (35 × 131 cm)
      Courtesy Mr. & Mrs. Melvin Sederstrom

Lake Geneva Hotel
(For Arthur L. Richards Company)
Lake Geneva, Wisconsin    1911
Window, art glass
43 × 21″ (109 × 53 cm)
Courtesy The School of Architecture and
Urban Planning, University of Wisconsin,
Milwaukee and Mr. & Mrs. Brian A. Spencer

80    Duplex Residence,
American System Built Houses
(For Arthur L. Richards Company)
Milwaukee, Wisconsin    1911-1917
Lithoprint
14⅞ × 12″ (38 × 31 cm)
Courtesy The Oak Park Public Library,
Grant Carpenter Manson Collection

Concrete bridge, Ravine Bluffs Subdivision
Glencoe, Illinois    1911
Colored pencil on illustration board
22 × 28″ (56 × 76 cm)
Courtesy Mr. & Mrs. John D. Randall

82    Sherman H. Booth Residence, Scheme 1
      Glencoe, Illinois    1911
      Colored pencil on illustration board
      21⅝ × 32″ (55 × 81 cm)
      Courtesy Mr. & Mrs. John D. Randall

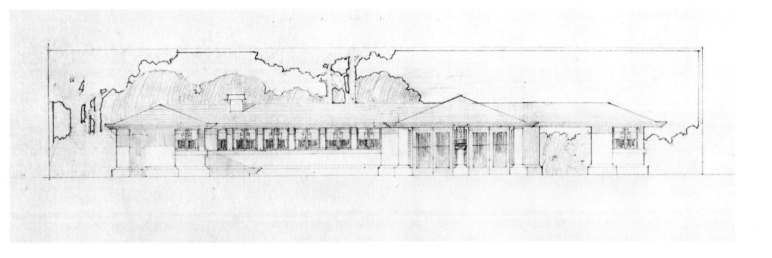

House for lot 22, Ravine Bluffs Subdivision
(For Sherman H. Booth)
Glencoe, Illinois    1911
Pencil on tracing paper
17 × 21½" (43 × 55 cm)
Courtesy Mr. & Mrs. John D. Randall

Sherman H. Booth Residence
Glencoe, Illinois    1912
Garage and stable design,
pencil on tracing paper
12¼ × 28¼" (31 × 72 cm)
Courtesy Mr. & Mrs. John D. Randall

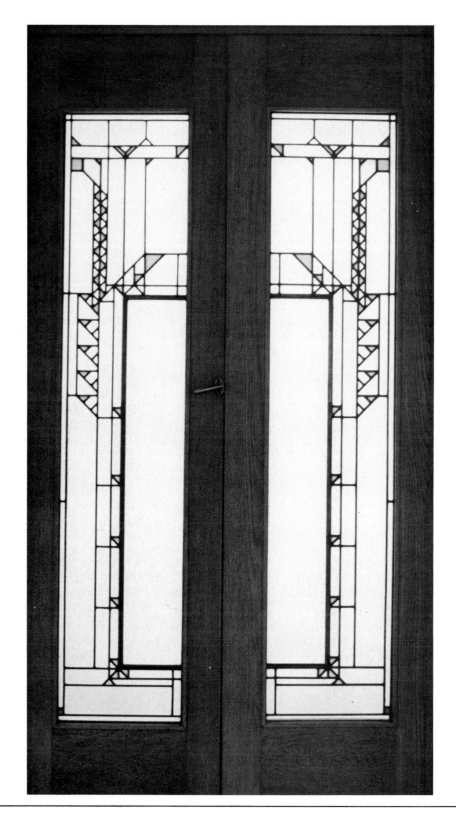

84    "Northome," Francis W. Little Residence
Deephaven, Minnesota    1912
Reconstruction of living room wall lamp,
oak and glass
32⅛ × 7 × 11" (82 × 18 × 28 cm)
Courtesy Edgar Allen Tafel,
executed by David Miller

"Northome," Francis W. Little Residence
Deephaven, Minnesota    1912
Doors, oak with leaded glass
77¼ × 41¾ × 1¾" (197 × 106 × 4 cm)
Courtesy The Metropolitan Museum of Art

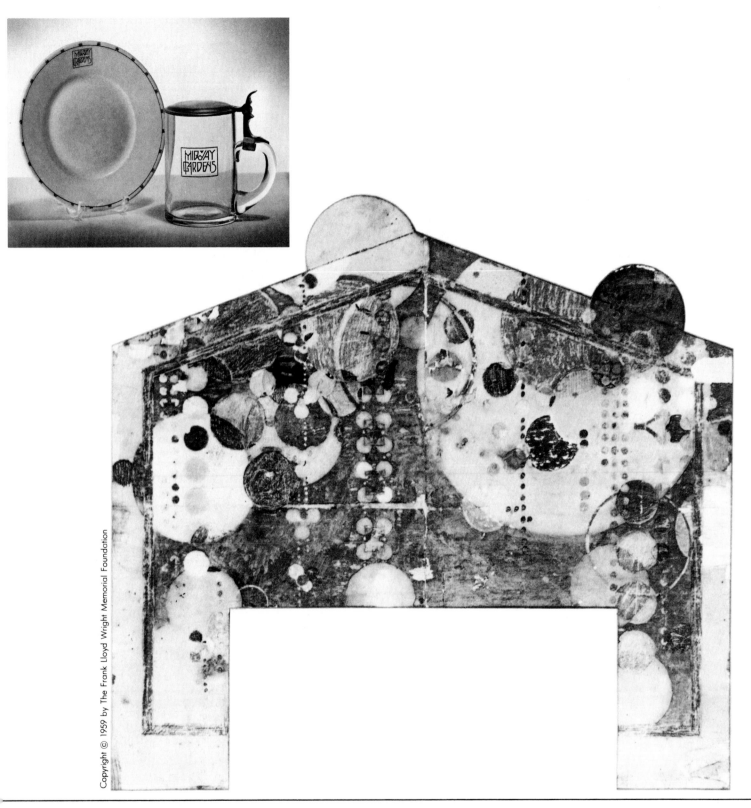

Top
Midway Gardens
Chicago, Illinois    1913
Luncheon plates, china
7½" (19 cm) diameter
Courtesy George Talbot
Beer stein, glass and metal
5⅛ × 3⅛" (13 × 8 cm)
Courtesy Jack W. Strand

Bottom
Midway Gardens
Chicago, Illinois    1913
City by the sea mural
Courtesy The Frank Lloyd Wright Memorial
Foundation

86        Imperial Hotel
Tokyo, Japan    1915
Ornament, terra cotta
8 × 8½" (20 × 22 cm)
Courtesy The State University of New York,
Buffalo, Gift of Edgar A. Tafel

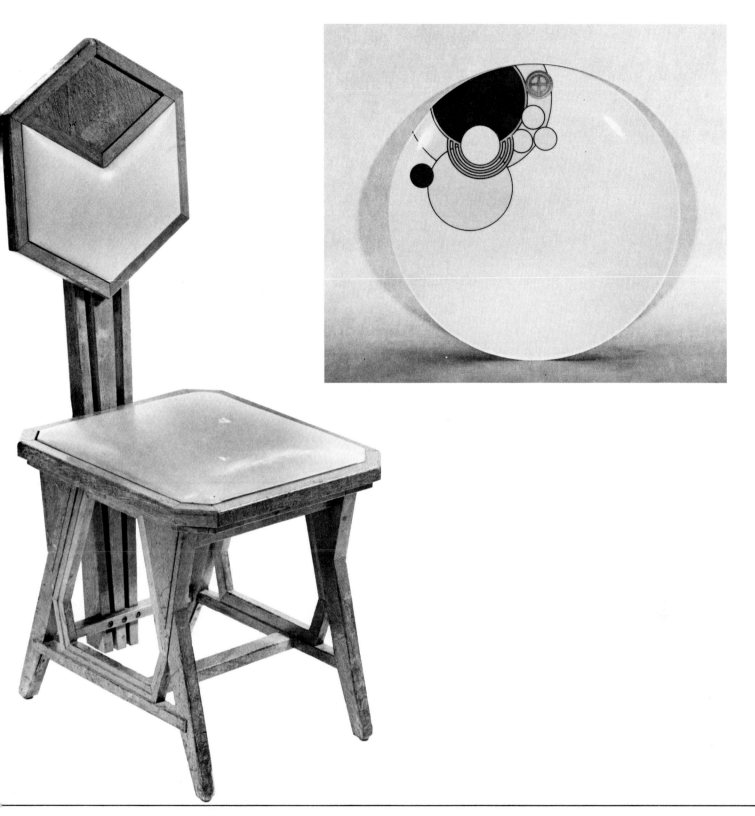

Imperial Hotel
Tokyo, Japan    1915
Dining chair, elm with upholstery
(originally with caning)
37½ × 15½ × 18" (95 × 39 × 46 cm)
Gift of The Frank Lloyd Wright
Society of Japan

Imperial Hotel
Tokyo, Japan    1916
Chinaware, Noritake china with
applied design
Courtesy Donald G. Kalec

88    F. C. Bogk Residence
Milwaukee, Wisconsin    1916
Living room scheme,
colored pencil on tracing paper
14 × 18″ (36 × 46 cm)
Courtesy Mr. & Mrs. Robert L. Jacobson

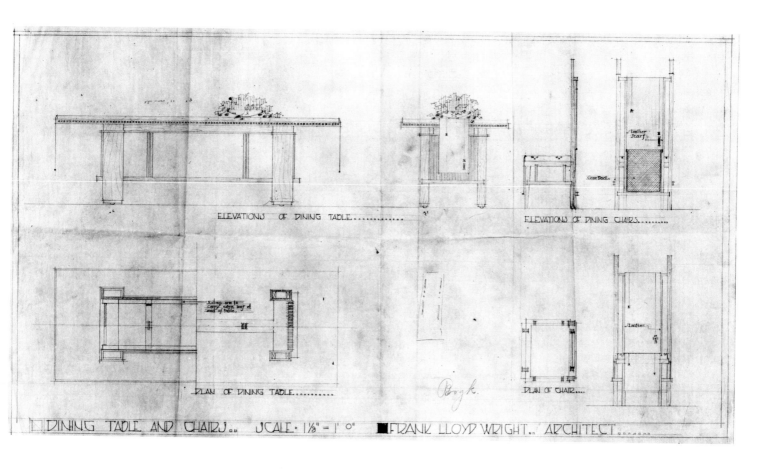

ELEVATIONS OF DINING TABLE..............

ELEVATIONS OF DINING CHAIRS.........

PLAN OF DINING TABLE............

Bogk.

PLAN OF CHAIR....

DINING TABLE AND CHAIRS.. SCALE·1⅛"=1'0" ■FRANK LLOYD WRIGHT.. ARCHITECT.

F. C. Bogk Residence
Milwaukee, Wisconsin    1916
Dining room table and chairs,
pencil on tracing paper
18¼ × 32½" (46 × 83 cm)
Courtesy Mr. & Mrs. Robert L. Jacobson

89

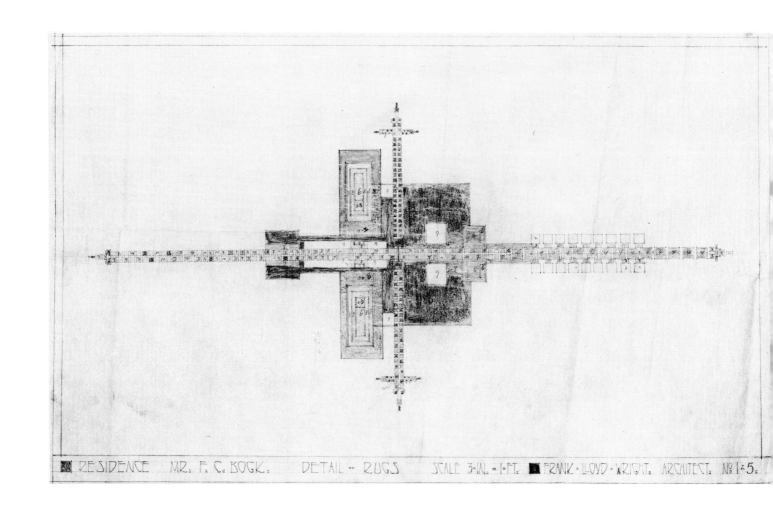

RESIDENCE MR. F. C. BOGK. DETAIL - RUGS SCALE 3-IN. = 1-FT. FRANK · LLOYD · WRIGHT. ARCHITECT. Nº 1 - 5.

**90**    F. C. Bogk Residence
Milwaukee, Wisconsin    1916
Entry stairs rug detail, colored
pencil on tracing paper
22 × 34¾" (56 × 88 cm)
Courtesy Mr. & Mrs. Robert L. Jacobson

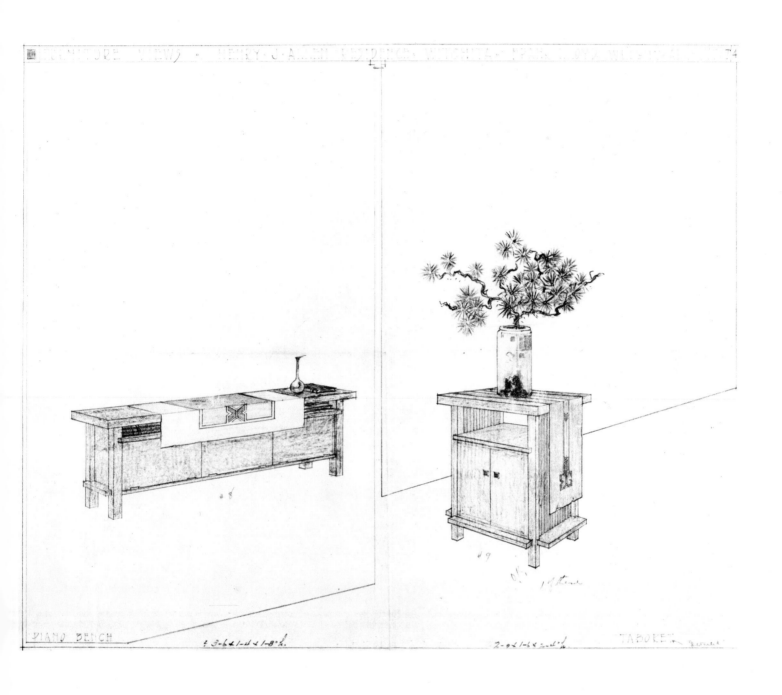

PIANO BENCH

TABOURET

Henry J. Allen Residence
Wichita, Kansas    1917
Piano bench and tabouret designs,
colored pencil on tracing paper
14⅝ × 17⅞" (37 × 45 cm)
Courtesy Mr. & Mrs. Robert L. Jacobson

92    Doheny Ranch Resort house
Los Angeles, California    1921
Courtesy The Frank Lloyd Wright Memorial
Foundation

"La Miniatura"
Mrs. George Millard Residence
Pasadena, California    1923
Courtesy The Frank Lloyd Wright Memorial
Foundation

**94**   Nakoma Basin Indian sculptures
Madison, Wisconsin   1924
Terra cotta with platinum glaze
Nakoma: 15¾″ (40 cm);
Nakomis: 12¼″ (31 cm)
Courtesy The Elvehjem Art Center,
University of Wisconsin, Madison

Stephen M. B. Hunt Residence
Oshkosh, Wisconsin   1917
Window, art glass
30 × 17⅝″ (76 × 45 cm)
Courtesy Mr. & Mrs. Robert N. Strass

Table lamp    1976 (Original design 1924)                                    95
Oak with fabric shade
20⅛ × 14 × 16″ (51 × 36 × 41 cm)
Courtesy Mr. & Mrs. Brian A. Spencer

96    National Life Insurance Company
(For A. M. Johnson)
Chicago, Illinois    1924
Courtesy The Frank Lloyd Wright Memorial
Foundation

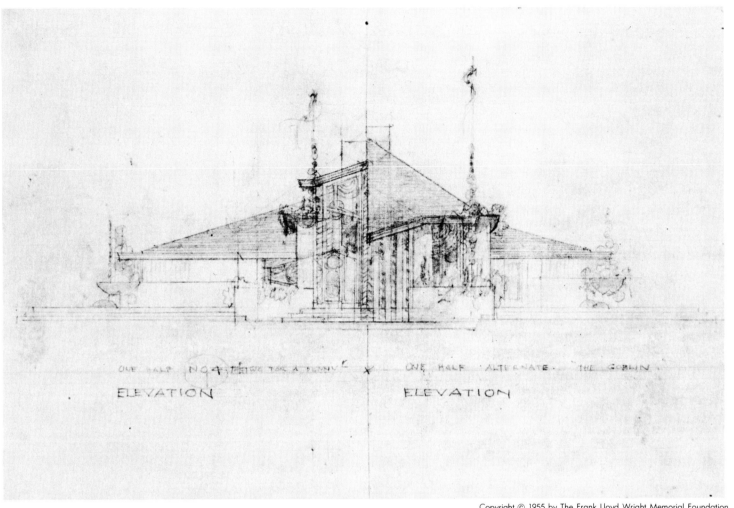

ONE HALF (NOT) THEATER FOR A PLAY X ONE HALF ALTERNATE THE GOBLIN

ELEVATION          ELEVATION

"Kinder Symphony," Oak Park Playhouse
Oak Park, Illinois    1926
Courtesy The Frank Lloyd Wright Memorial
Foundation

98

St. Mark's Tower
New York, New York    1929
Courtesy The Frank Lloyd Wright Memorial
Foundation

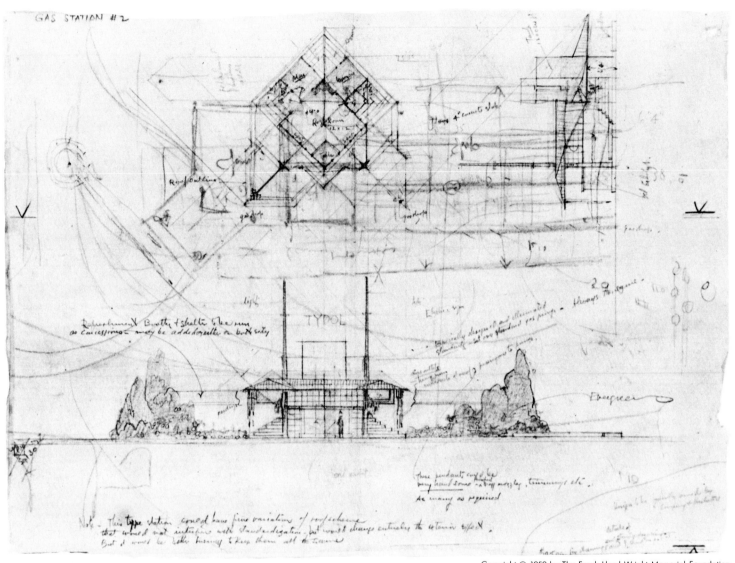

Standardized gas station #2    1931
Broadacre City Project
Courtesy The Frank Lloyd Wright Memorial
Foundation

100      "Fallingwater," Edgar J. Kaufmann
Residence
Bear Run, Pennsylvania     1935
Photograph courtesy Hedrich-Blessing

Taliesin West
Scottsdale, Arizona    1937
Photograph courtesy Hedrich-Blessing

102

Administration Building
S. C. Johnson and Son, Co.
Racine, Wisconsin    1936
Photograph courtesy S. C. Johnson and Son

S. C. Johnson and Son, Co.
Racine, Wisconsin    1936
Three-legged chair and desk, metal with
upholstering and metal with oak
35¼ × 18 × 21½" (90 × 46 × 55 cm)
Courtesy S. C. Johnson and Son

A COUNTRY DWELLING FOR MR AND MRS HERBERT F JOHNS
WINDY POINT RACINE WISCONS
FRANK LLOYD WRIGHT ARCHITE

104 "Wingspread,"
Herbert F. Johnson Residence
Wind Point, Racine, Wisconsin    1937
Courtesy The Frank Lloyd Wright Memorial
Foundation

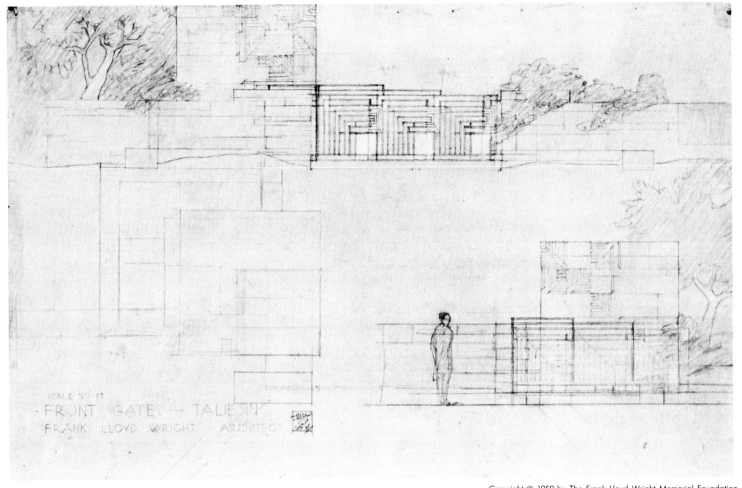

SCALE 1/4" FT
FRONT GATE — TALIESIN
FRANK LLOYD WRIGHT / ARCHITECT

Taliesin
Spring Green, Wisconsin     1939
Front gate
Courtesy The Frank Lloyd Wright Memorial
Foundation

106     Lloyd Lewis Residence
Libertyville, Illinois    1939
Courtesy The Frank Lloyd Wright Memorial
Foundation

Crystal Heights Hotel, Shipping Center and
Apartments
Washington, D. C.     1939
Courtesy The Frank Lloyd Wright Memorial
Foundation

FRANK LLOYD WRIGHT

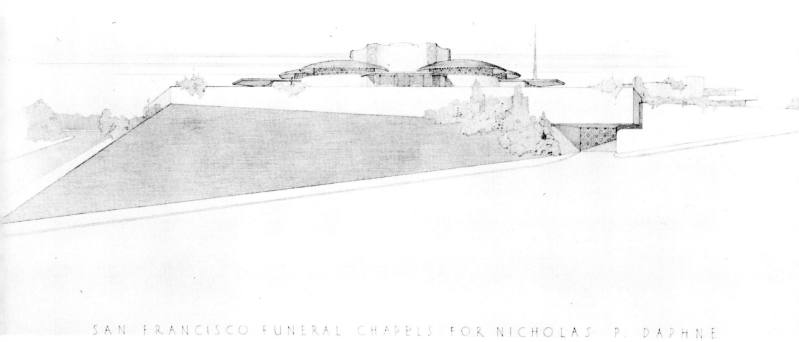

SAN FRANCISCO FUNERAL CHAPELS FOR NICHOLAS P. DAPHNE

108    Daphne Funeral Chapels
San Francisco, California    1945
Courtesy The Frank Lloyd Wright Memorial
Foundation

COUNTRY CLUB FOR HUNTINGTON HARTFORD HOLLYWOOD
FRANK LLOYD WRIGHT ARCHITECT

Huntington Hartford Play Resort, Sports Club
Hollywood, California    1947
Courtesy The Frank Lloyd Wright Memorial
Foundation

110   Clarence Sondern Residence
Kansas City, Missouri    1939
Chairs, cypress plywood with upholstering
29 × 22 × 25″ (74 × 56 × 64 cm) and
28 × 18 × 21″ (71 × 46 × 53 cm)
Courtesy The Warehouse (A. D. German
Warehouse)

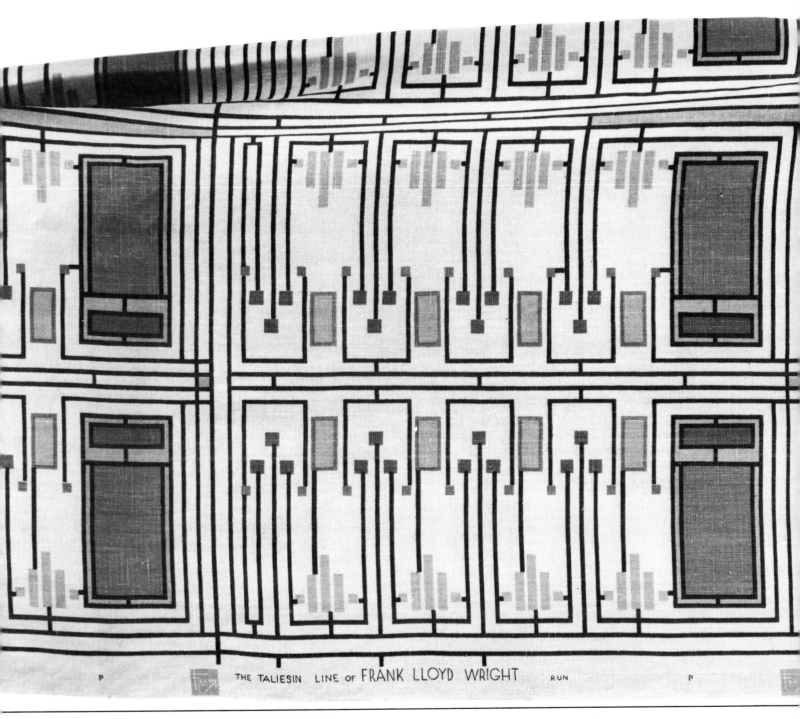

THE TALIESIN LINE of FRANK LLOYD WRIGHT    RUN

Wallpaper and fabric    1955
(For F. Schumacher & Son)
Paper and cotton
Courtesy Mr. & Mrs. Irvin Penkalski

111

112    "Four Square" Furniture for
Heritage Henredon    1955
Oak with upholstering
Arm chair: 44 × 19¾ × 19⅜"
(112 × 50 × 49 cm)
Hassock: 18¾ × 16 × 16"
(48 × 41 × 41 cm)
Tall back chair: 29¾ × 25¾ × 22"
(74 × 65 × 56 cm)
Courtesy The Frank Lloyd Wright Memorial
Foundation

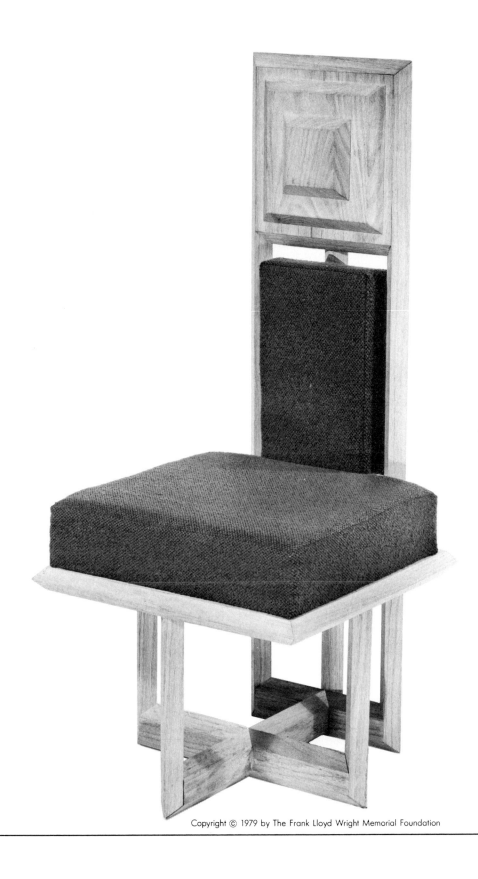

WISCONSIN RIVER TERRACE RESTAURANT
FOR THE TALIESIN VALLEY , SPRING GREEN , WISCONSIN
FRANK LLOYD WRIGHT ARCHITECT

**114**    "The Spring Green,"
riverview terrace restaurant
Spring Green, Wisconsin    1953
Colored pencil on paper
18 × 36" (46 × 91 cm)
Delineated by Lynn Anderson

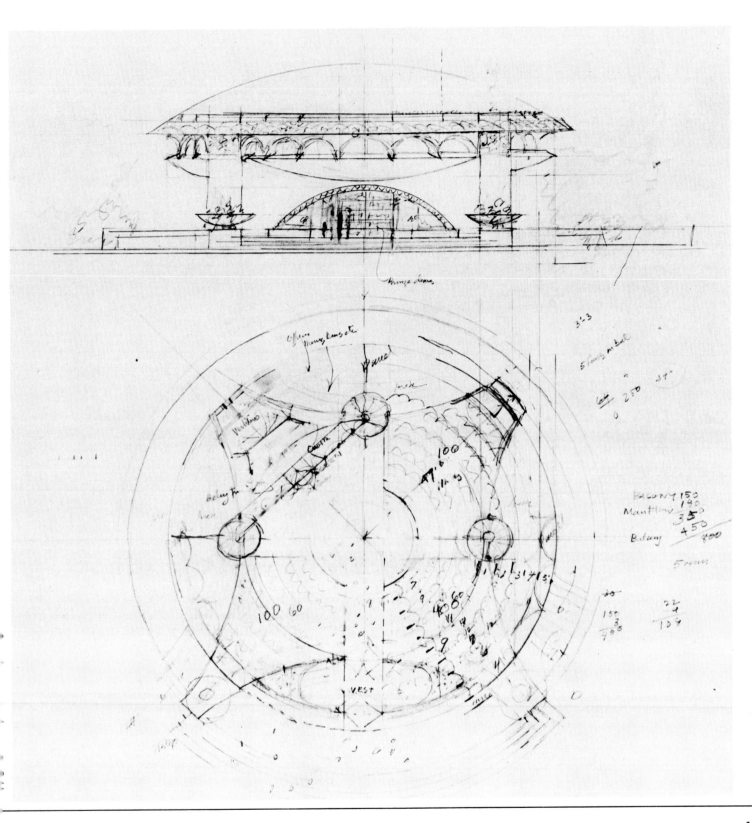

Annunciation Greek Orthodox Church
Wauwatosa, Wisconsin     1956
Courtesy The Frank Lloyd Wright Memorial
Foundation

# P A R K E R   N .   B E R R Y   ( 1 8 8 8 - 1 9 1 8 )

Born in Princeton, Illinois, Parker N. Berry was the son of a
local building contractor. After two years at the architectural
school of the University of Illinois, Berry left in 1909 to gain a
first-hand knowledge of contemporary American design in
the architectural offices of Chicago. Berry was hired as a
draftsman by Louis H. Sullivan in 1909, and after the departure of George Grant Elmslie, the 21-year-old Berry became
Sullivan's chief draftsman. Although he received his architect's license in 1912, Berry remained with Sullivan for over
eight years. Leaving Sullivan's office in 1917 after arguments
with Sullivan over his independent commissions, Berry
opened his own firm in Chicago. During the last 19 months
of his life, Berry designed several commissions and projects
which bear the strong influence of both Sullivan and the
style of Purcell and Elmslie. His untimely death in 1918 per-
mits only speculation as to how his independent style might
have developed.

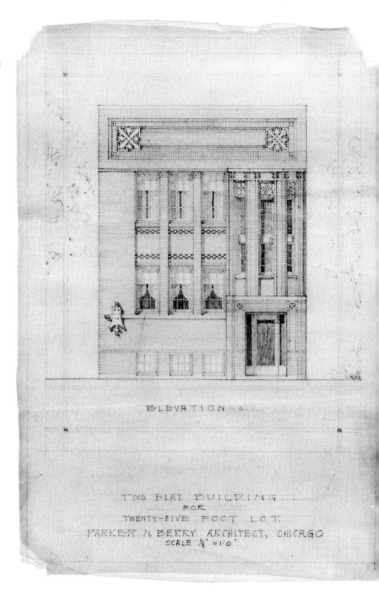

Two-flat building for twenty-five foot lot
no date
Pencil on tracing paper
8¼ × 5½" (21 × 14 cm)
Courtesy The Burnham Library,
The Art Institute of Chicago

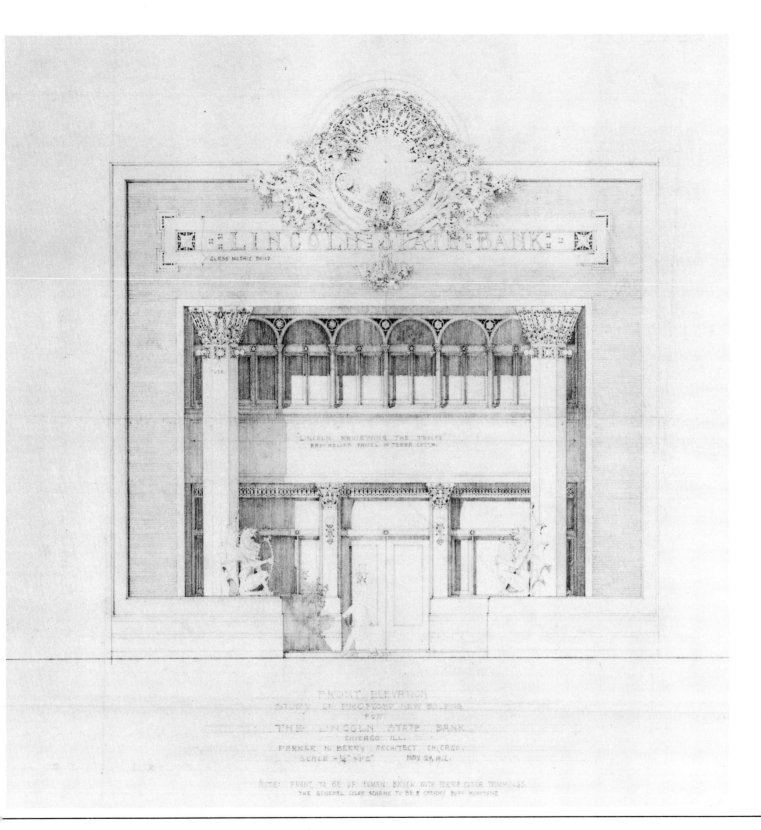

Lincoln State Bank
Chicago, Illinois 1912
Pencil on tracing paper
13 × 20¼" (33 × 57 cm)
Courtesy The Burnham Library,
The Art Institute of Chicago

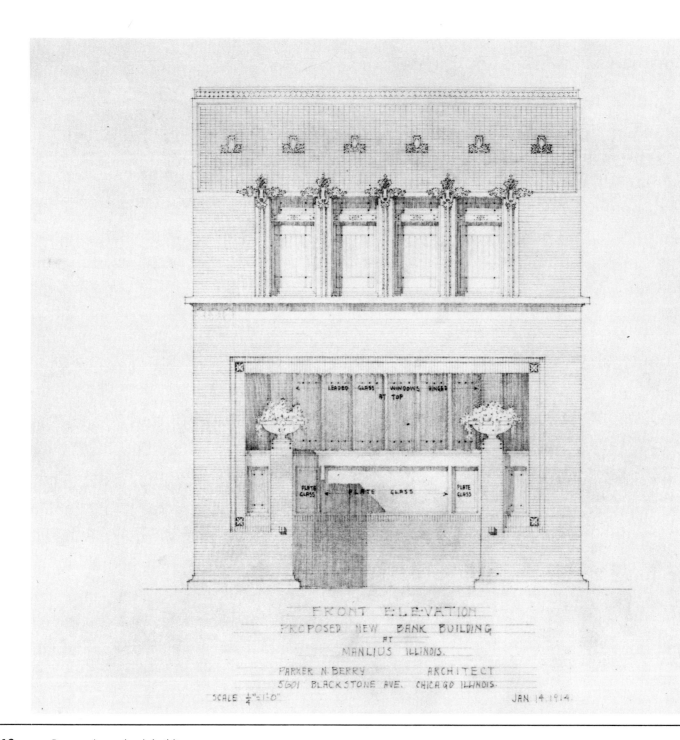

FRONT ELEVATION
PROPOSED NEW BANK BUILDING
AT
MANLIUS ILLINOIS.

PARKER N BERRY          ARCHITECT
5601 BLACKSTONE AVE. CHICAGO ILLINOIS.
SCALE ¼"=1'-0"                    JAN 14 1914

118     Proposed new bank building
        Manlius, Illinois    1914
        Pencil on tracing paper
        12¼ × 15" (31 × 38 cm)
        Courtesy The Burnham Library,
        The Art Institute of Chicago

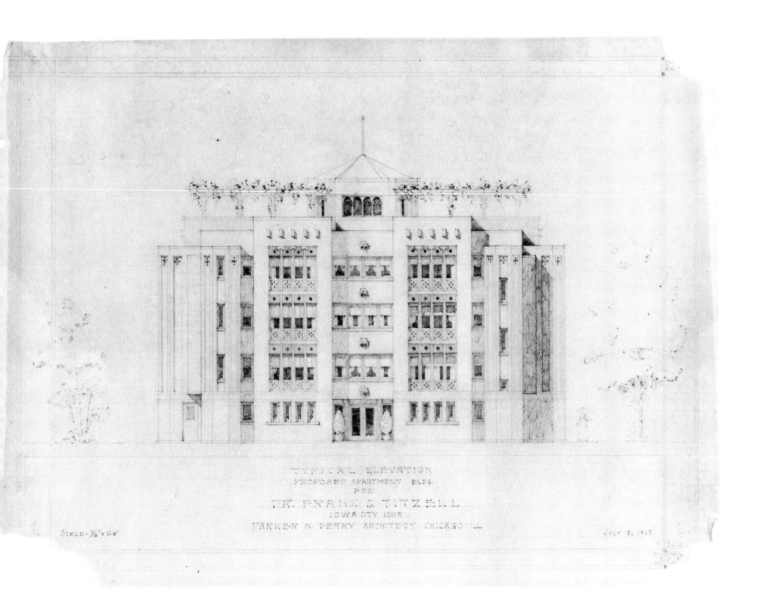

Proposed apartment building
(For Dr. Frank C. Titzell)
Iowa City, Iowa    1915
Pencil on tracing paper
6½ × 8¾" (17 × 22 cm)
Courtesy The Burnham Library,
The Art Institute of Chicago

# PURCELL, FEICK AND ELMSLIE (1909-1913)

## WILLIAM GRAY PURCELL (1880-1964)
## GEORGE FEICK, JR. (1881-1945)
## GEORGE GRANT ELMSLIE (1871-1952)

George Grant Elmslie immigrated to the United States from Scotland in 1884 and began his architectural apprenticeship in the office of William LeBaron Jenney in Chicago. Then in 1887, he worked, along with Frank Lloyd Wright and George Maher, in the office of Joseph Lyman Silsbee.

William Gray Purcell, raised in Oak Park, Illinois, by his grandparents, received his architectural training at Cornell University and apprenticed in the offices of Adler & Sullivan and John Gallen Howard in Berkeley, California, before entering into partnership with former Cornell classmate, George Feick, Jr., in Minneapolis.

Elmslie joined Adler & Sullivan's firm in 1889 with a recommendation from Wright and in 1894, after Wright's departure, became chief draftsman of the firm. Elmslie maintained this position for close to fifteen years, leaving during construction of the Harold C. Bradley Residence in Madison, Wisconsin, in 1909. Taking with him the furniture designs, decorations, and interior details, Elmslie formed a partnership with Purcell and Feick in Minneapolis. Purcell and Feick had already established a strong practice and the addition of the senior Elmslie only contributed to the reputation of the firm. This new association produced a very active practice designing residences, offices, public buildings, factories, and stores throughout California, Connecticut, Massachusetts, the Midwest, and Pennsylvania. One of the high points of the firm was the superbly detailed Merchants Bank of Winona, Minnesota, in 1911-1912.

In 1913, George Feick, Jr., left the firm, and Purcell and Elmslie continued the practice until the partnership dissolved around 1922. This later period of partnership produced a series of small Midwest banks, though none equaled the articulation of the earlier one in Winona.

Because of poor health, Purcell entered semiretirement and moved to Portland, Oregon; eventually he retired to

Pasadena, California. Elmslie maintained a private practice until the Depression, when he found it necessary to work for William S. Hutton, Architect. He spent the end of his career in semiretirement, with occasional writing and informal speaking.

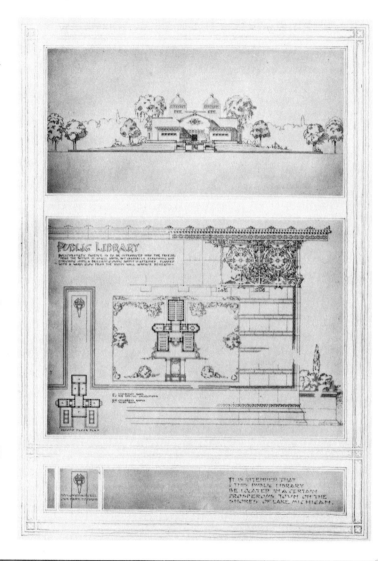

William Gray Purcell
A town library    circa 1903
Ink on paper
17 × 11¾" (43 × 30 cm)
Courtesy Northwest Architectural Archives,
University of Minnesota

Purcell & Feick, 1907-1909
First National Bank of Winona
Winona, Minnesota    1907
Pencil on tracing paper
6¼ × 13⅝″ (16 × 35 cm)
Courtesy Northwest Architectural Archives,
University of Minnesota

122   Purcell & Feick, 1907-1909
Stewart Memorial Church
Minneapolis, Minnesota    1909
Colored pencil on tracing paper
9 × 6" (23 × 15 cm)
Courtesy Northwest Architectural Archives,
University of Minnesota

Purcell & Feick, 1907-1909
Stewart Memorial Church
Minneapolis, Minnesota    1909
Colored pencil on tracing paper
8¾ × 15¾" (22 × 40 cm)
Courtesy Northwest Architectural Archives,
University of Minnesota

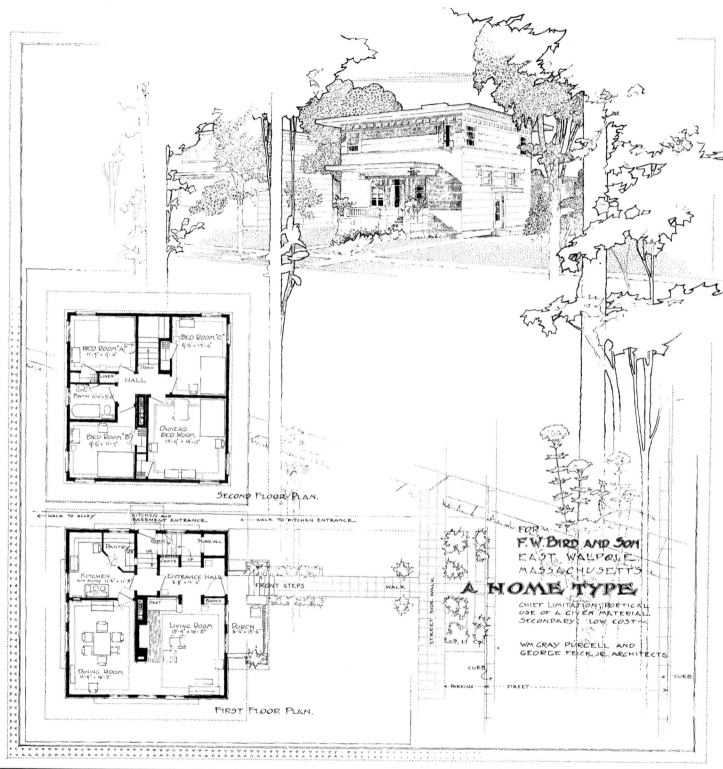

Within the drawing:

BED ROOM "A"
11'-7" x 9'-4"

BED ROOM "C"
9'-8" x 13'-4"

DOWN

LINEN

HALL

BATH 6'-0" x 5'-0"

BED ROOM "B"
9'-6" x 11'-7"

OWNERS BED ROOM
13'-9" x 14'-0"

SECOND FLOOR PLAN.

WALK TO ALLEY

KITCHEN AND BASEMENT ENTRANCE

WALK TO KITCHEN ENTRANCE

PANTRY

DOWN

STORE-ALL

UP

COATS

UP

KITCHEN
with pantry 11'-6" x 11'-3"

ENTRANCE HALL
6'-8" x 11'-6"

FRONT STEPS

WALK

BOOKS

SEAT

LIVING ROOM
13'-9" x 16'-8"

PORCH
6'-6" x 13'-6"

DINING ROOM
11'-9" x 16'-7"

FIRST FLOOR PLAN.

STREET SIDE WALK

FOR
F. W. BIRD AND SON
EAST WALPOLE
MASSACHUSETTS

A HOME TYPE

CHIEF LIMITATION: POETICAL
USE OF A GIVEN MATERIAL
SECONDARY: LOW COST

WM. GRAY PURCELL AND
GEORGE FEICK JR. ARCHITECTS

CURB

PARKING

STREET

CURB

124    Purcell & Feick, 1907-1909
A home type for F. W. Bird and Son
East Walpole, Massachusetts    no date
Ink on heavy paper
17½ × 18⅛" (45 × 46 cm)
Courtesy Northwest Architectural Archives,
University of Minnesota

St. Paul's Methodist Church
Cedar Rapids, Iowa      1910
Ink on linen
25¾ × 31¼" (65 × 79 cm)
Courtesy Northwest Architectural Archives,
University of Minnesota

FIRST NATIONAL BANK RHINELANDER

126     First National Bank
        Rhinelander, Wisconsin     1911
        Ink on linen
        6½ × 11⅜" (17 × 29 cm)
        Courtesy Northwest Architectural Archives,
        University of Minnesota

First National Bank
Rhinelander, Wisconsin    1911
Skylight sections, art glass
55¼ × 27¼″ (140 × 69 cm)
Courtesy Mr. & Mrs. Brian A. Spencer and
a private collection

**128**  First National Bank
Mankato, Minnesota    1911
Ink on linen
18½ × 27" (47 × 69 cm)
Courtesy Northwest Architectural Archives,
University of Minnesota

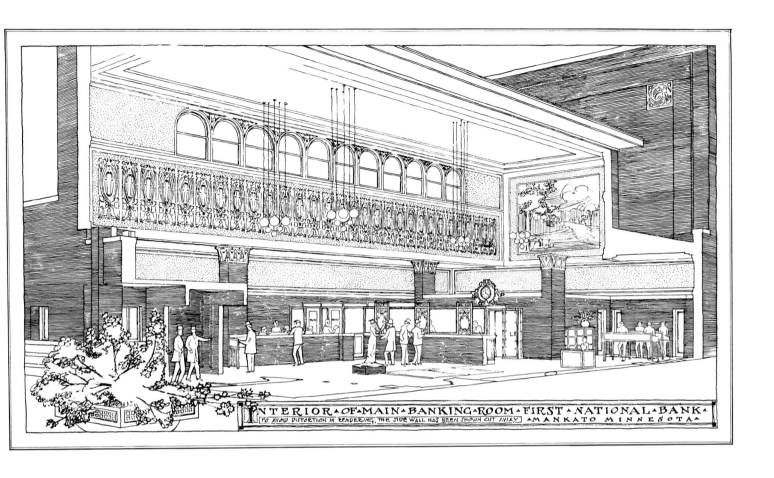

INTERIOR·OF·MAIN·BANKING·ROOM·FIRST·NATIONAL·BANK·
[TO AVOID DISTORTION IN RENDERING, THE SIDE WALL HAS BEEN SHOWN CUT AWAY]·MANKATO MINNESOTA·

First National Bank
Mankato, Minnesota    1911
Ink on linen
10⅛ × 18⅛" (26 × 46 cm)
Courtesy Northwest Architectural Archives,
University of Minnesota

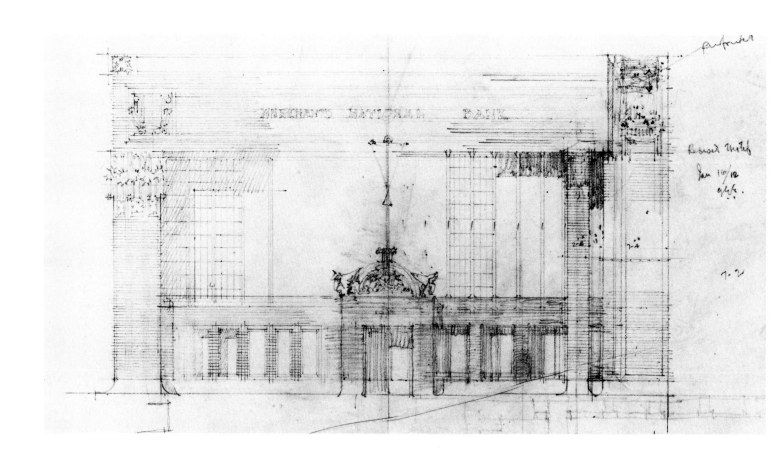

130    Merchants Bank of Winona
Winona, Minnesota    1911-1912
Pencil on tracing paper
11 × 8½" (28 × 22 cm)
Courtesy Northwest Architectural Archives,
University of Minnesota

Merchants Bank of Winona
Winona, Minnesota    1911-1912
Photograph courtesy of Northwest
Architectural Archives, University of
Minnesota

132

Babson Edison Shop
Chicago, Illinois    1912
Photograph and graphic design for the
*Western Architect*
Courtesy Northwest Architectural Archives,
University of Minnesota

Purcell and Elmslie, 1913-1922
Madison State Bank
Madison, Minnesota    1913
Photograph courtesy Northwest
Architectural Archives,
University of Minnesota

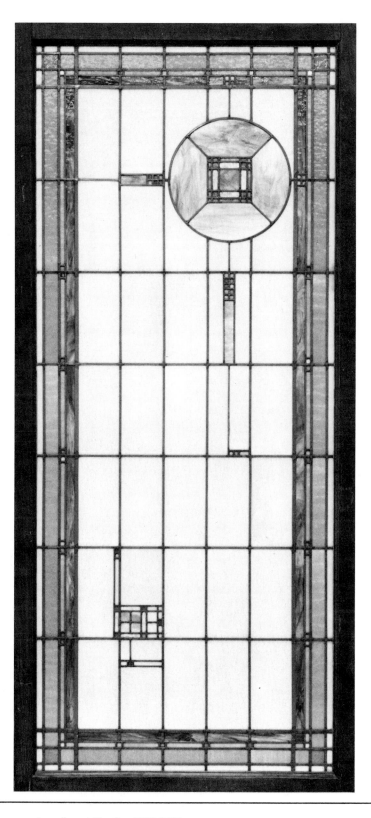

Purcell and Elmslie, 1913-1922
Madison State Bank
Madison, Minnesota    1913
Skylight section, art glass
70 × 32″ (178 × 81 cm)
Courtesy The Bertrand and Margaret
Goderstad Collection

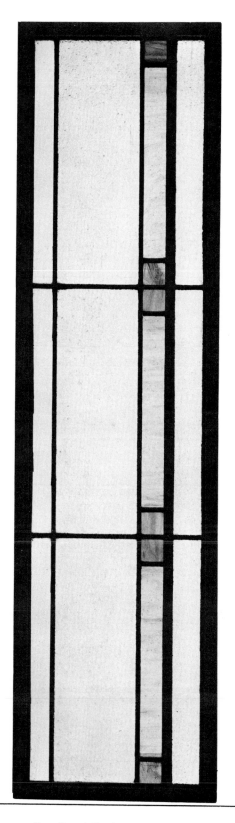

Purcell and Elmslie, 1913-1922
Madison State Bank
Madison, Minnesota    1913
Windows, art glass
73 × 23″ (185 × 58 cm)
Courtesy Mr. & Mrs. Leo Schumacher

Purcell and Elmslie, 1913-1922
Land Office Building
Stanley, Wisconsin    1916
Windows, art glass
12 × 46″ (31 × 117 cm)
Courtesy Mr. & Mrs. Brian A. Spencer

# FRANCIS BARRY BYRNE (1883-1967)

Francis Barry Byrne's training in architecture began in 1902 in Frank Lloyd Wright's Oak Park studio. Between 1906 and 1908 he worked on two of Wright's important early commissions: Unity Temple in Oak Park and the Avery Coonley Residence in Riverside, Illinois. In 1908 he left Wright's office to establish a practice in Seattle, Washington, with a former member of the Wright studio, Andrew Willatzen. In 1914, Byrne returned to Illinois to take over the practice of Walter Burley Griffin, who was leaving for Australia to build the new capitol at Canberra. Griffin and his wife, Marion Mahoney Griffin, were senior members of the Oak Park studio at the time Byrne was in apprenticeship there. They contributed to the formation of his mature style, which tended to be more space enclosing than the work of Wright. Byrne traveled in Europe in 1925 and was impressed by the contemporary architecture he saw there, especially the work of the German and Dutch Expressionists. This resulted in a change in his style—in particular to a more dramatic massing of forms, which gave his work a new, more formalistic approach.

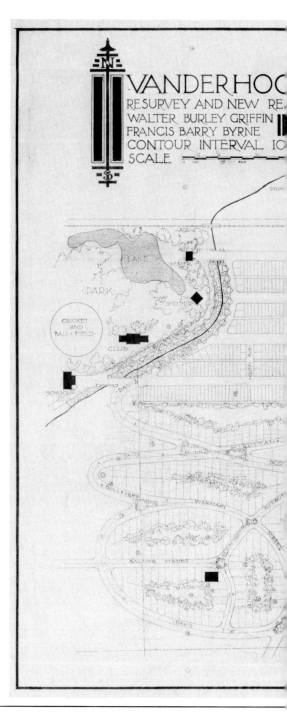

Town plan
Vanderhoof, British Columbia    1915
Ink on linen
28⅞ × 45⅞" (73 × 117 cm)
Courtesy Annette Cremin Byrne

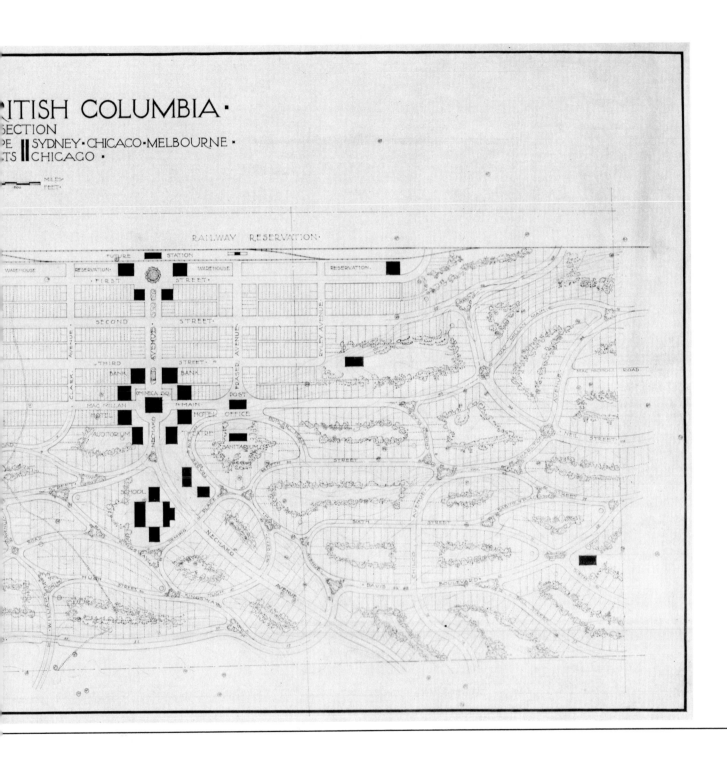

BRITISH COLUMBIA·

SECTION

SYDNEY·CHICAGO·MELBOURNE·

CHICAGO·

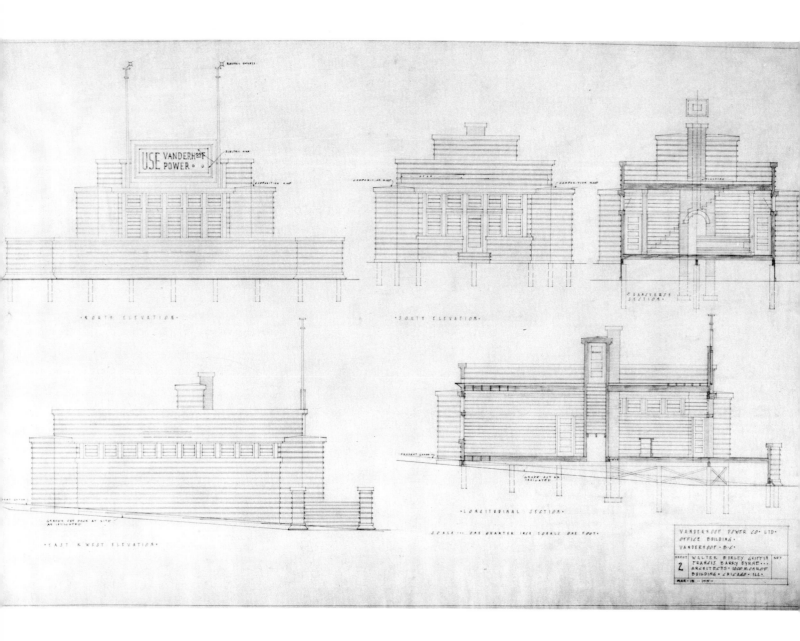

**138**　Vanderhoof Power Company, Ltd.
Vanderhoof, British Columbia　1915
Ink on linen
24½ × 36″ (62 × 91 cm)
Courtesy Annette Cremin Byrne

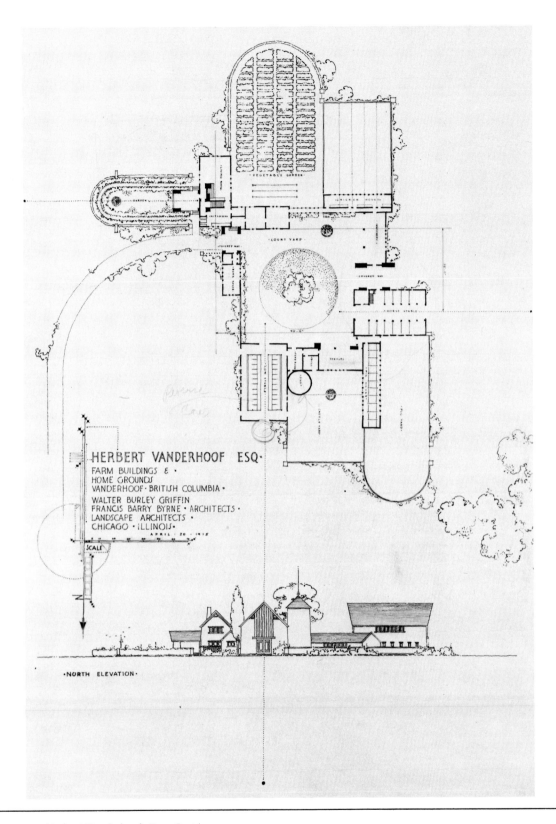

HERBERT VANDERHOOF ESQ·
FARM BUILDINGS &·
HOME GROUNDS·
VANDERHOOF·BRITISH COLUMBIA·
WALTER BURLEY GRIFFIN
FRANCIS BARRY BYRNE · ARCHITECTS ·
LANDSCAPE ARCHITECTS ·
CHICAGO ·ILLINOIS·
APRIL·20·1915

SCALE

·NORTH ELEVATION·

Herbert Vanderhoof, Esq., Residence
Vanderhoof, British Columbia    1915
Ink on linen
41⅞ × 23⅛″ (106 × 59 cm)
Courtesy Annette Cremin Byrne

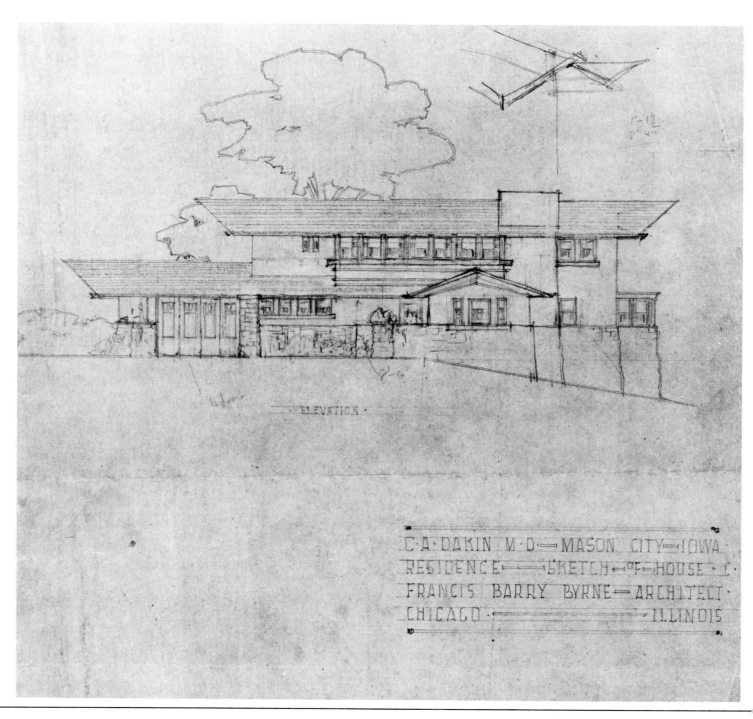

· ELEVATION ·

C·A·DAKIN·M·D — MASON CITY — IOWA
RESIDENCE — SKETCH · OF · HOUSE · C
FRANCIS BARRY BYRNE — ARCHITECT
CHICAGO · — ILLINOIS

140     C. A. Dakin Residence
Mason City, Iowa    1917
Pencil on tracing paper
15½ × 16½" (39 × 42 cm)
Courtesy Annette Cremin Byrne

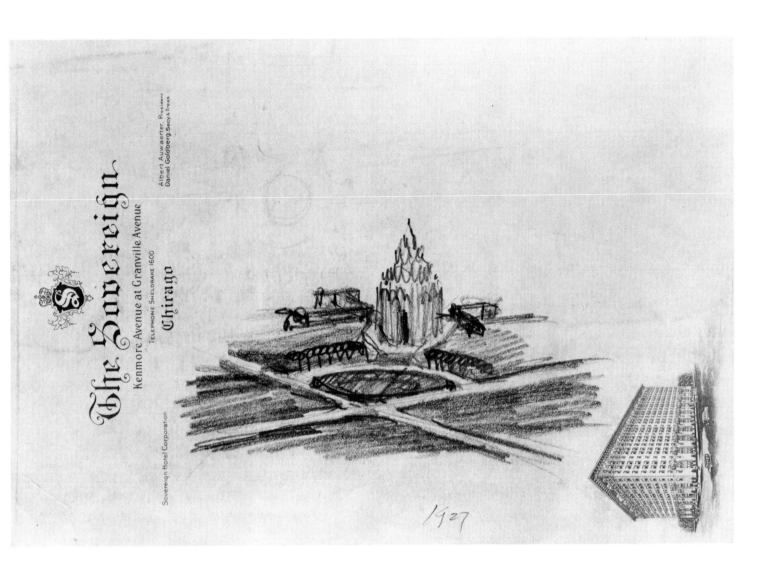

Unidentified cathedral study    1927
Pencil on "The Sovereign Hotel" stationery
7⅜ × 10⅝" (18 × 27 cm)
Courtesy Annette Cremin Byrne

142    Immaculata High School
       Chicago, Illinois    circa 1920
       Scheme 1, colored pencil on
       illustration board
       21 × 34" (53 × 86 cm)
       Courtesy Annette Cremin Byrne

United Theater
Minneapolis, Minnesota    no date
Browntone print
19⅛ × 18⅜″ (49 × 47 cm)
Courtesy Annette Cremin Byrne

143

144     Church of Christ the King
          Tulsa, Oklahoma    1926
          Courtesy Annette Cremin Byrne

Table and chairs, oak     no date
Table: 28 × 60 × 32¼"
(71 × 152 × 82 cm);
chairs: 37 × 20¼ × 20¼"
(94 × 51 × 51 cm)
Courtesy Annette Cremin Byrne

# ALPHONSO IANNELLI (1888-1965)

Born in Italy, Alphonso Iannelli came to America and settled in Newark, New Jersey, with his family in 1898. At the age of 17, he won a scholarship to study at the Art Students' League in New York City, where he won several prizes and various honors. He soon became an assistant in the studio of his teacher, Gutzon Borglum, and within a year established his own studio in New York. In 1907, Iannelli expanded into the more marketable field of commercial arts, producing designs for magazines such as *Harper's Weekly* and *The Ladies' Home Journal.* In 1910 he traveled to California and took a job designing weekly vaudeville posters for the lobby of the Orpheum Theater in Los Angeles. These posters provide the link to Frank Lloyd Wright and the Prairie architects. Frank Lloyd Wright's son, John, who attended the theater regularly, brought them to the attention of his father, and in 1914 Wright asked Iannelli to come to Chicago to work on the sculptural decoration for Midway Gardens. Iannelli worked with several of the Prairie architects, including Purcell and Elmslie and Barry Byrne through the 1930s. In addition to his activities as sculptor, painter, and teacher, Iannelli also worked on industrial and architectural design projects.

Orpheum Theater Poster of Claude and
Fanny Usher
Los Angeles, California    1910-1913
Tempera on paper
30 × 40" (76 × 102 cm)
Courtesy Chicago School of Architecture
Foundation

Present Skit.
"The Circus Girl"

MARIE & BILL
HART

Orpheum Theater Poster of
Marie and Bill Hart
Los Angeles, California   1910-1913
Tempera on paper
30 × 40″ (76 × 102 cm)
Courtesy Chicago School of Architecture
Foundation

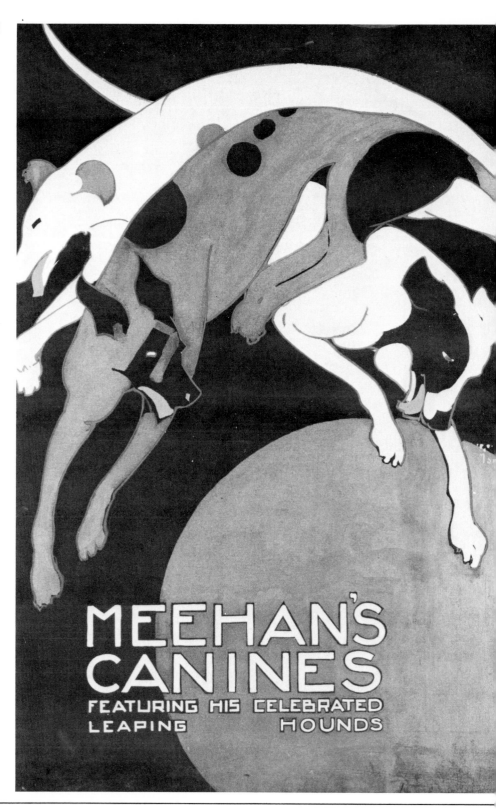

148

Orpheum Theater Poster of
Meehan's canines
Los Angeles, California    1910-1913
Tempera on paper
30 × 40″ (76 × 102 cm)
Courtesy Chicago School of Architecture
Foundation

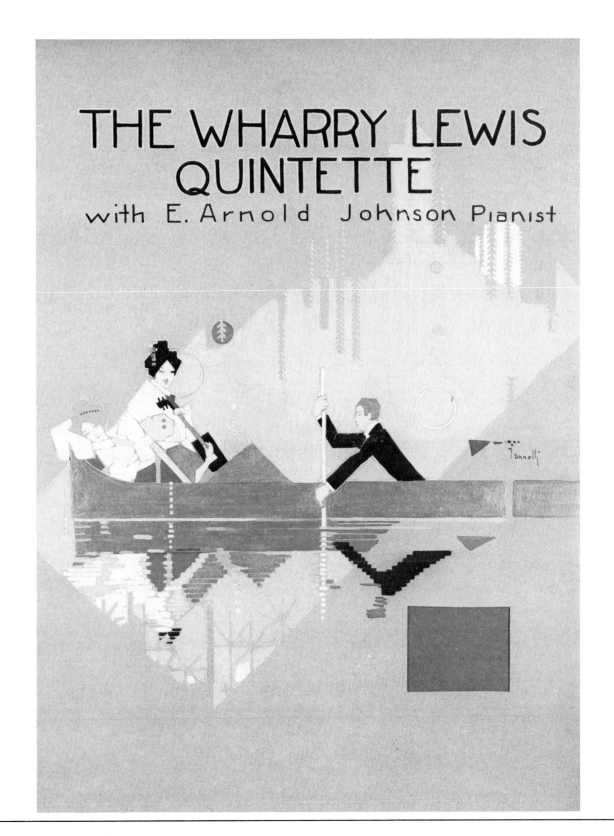

Orpheum Theater Poster of
The Wharry Lewis Quintette
Los Angeles, California    1910-1913
Tempera on paper
30 × 40″ (76 × 102 cm)
Courtesy Chicago School of Architecture
Foundation

150

Midway Gardens sculpture model
Chicago, Illinois    1914
Plaster
10⅝" (27 cm)
Courtesy Chicago School of Architecture
Foundation

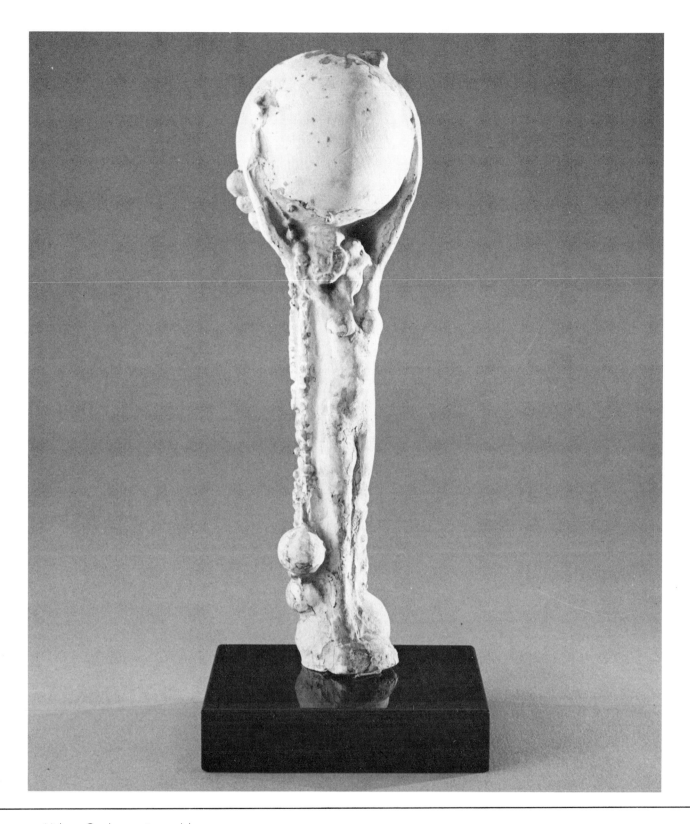

Midway Gardens sprite model
Chicago, Illinois      1914
Plaster
10⅜″ (26 cm)
Courtesy Chicago School of Architecture
Foundation

# WALTER BURLEY GRIFFIN (1876-1937)
# MARION MAHONEY GRIFFIN (1871-1962)

Born in Maywood, Illinois, and raised in Oak Park, Walter Burley Griffin studied architecture under Clifford Ricker at the University of Illinois. After graduation, Griffin joined the Steinway Hall group of architects for a few years before entering the employ of Frank Lloyd Wright at the Oak Park studio. Here, working in the Prairie idiom, he was free to develop a style noted for a distinctive vertical massing of forms as well as an interest in landscape architecture. After leaving Wright's employ in 1905, Griffin worked with several other Prairie school architects (including a partnership with Barry Byrne), and he undertook a variety of projects ranging from residential commissions to planning residential subdivisions, campus and city planning, including his prize-winning concept for the new federal capital at Canberra, Australia. It was in the Oak Park studio that Griffin met Marion Mahoney; they were married in 1911.

Born in Chicago, Marion Mahoney was one of the first women graduates of MIT. In 1895, she entered the Oak Park studio of Frank Lloyd Wright. She was best known for the renderings which she produced first for Wright and then for her husband. In addition, she designed furnishings for some of Wright's houses, as well as completing some of Wright's architectural designs while he was out of the country from 1909 to 1911.

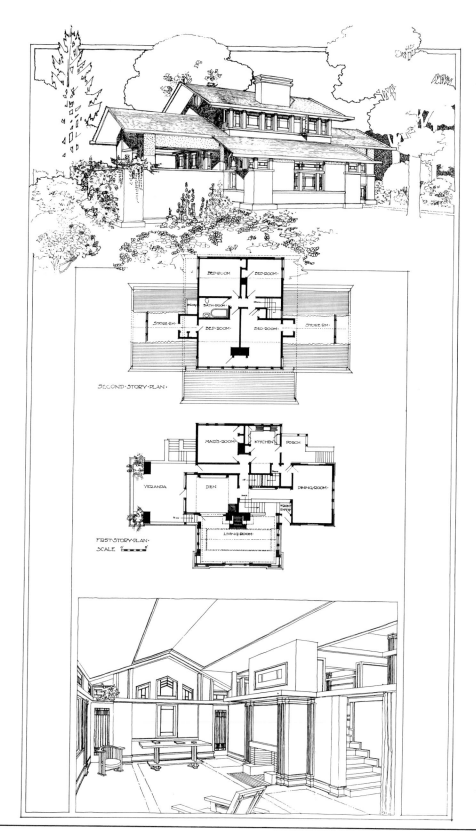

Ralph D. Griffin Residence
Edwardsville, Illinois    circa 1910
Ink on linen
41 × 21½" (104 × 55 cm)
Courtesy Northwestern University

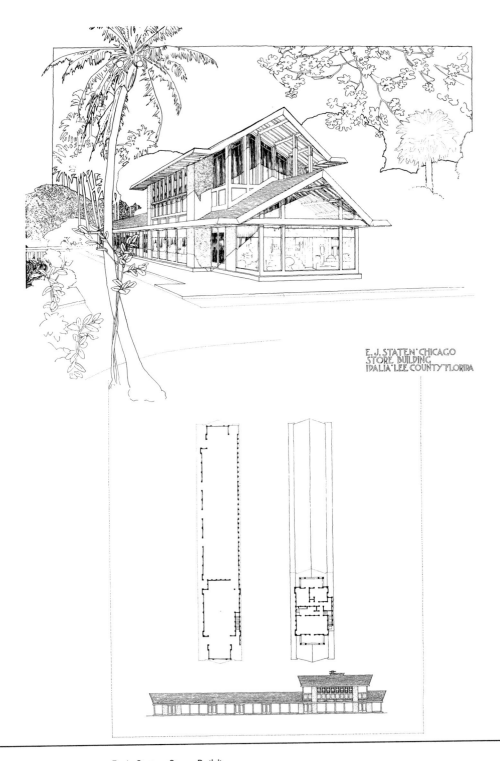

E. J. STATEN·CHICAGO
STORE· BUILDING
IDALIA·LEE COUNTY·FLORIDA

154

E. J. Staten Store Building
Idalia, Lee County, Florida    1911
Ink on linen
Courtesy Northwestern University

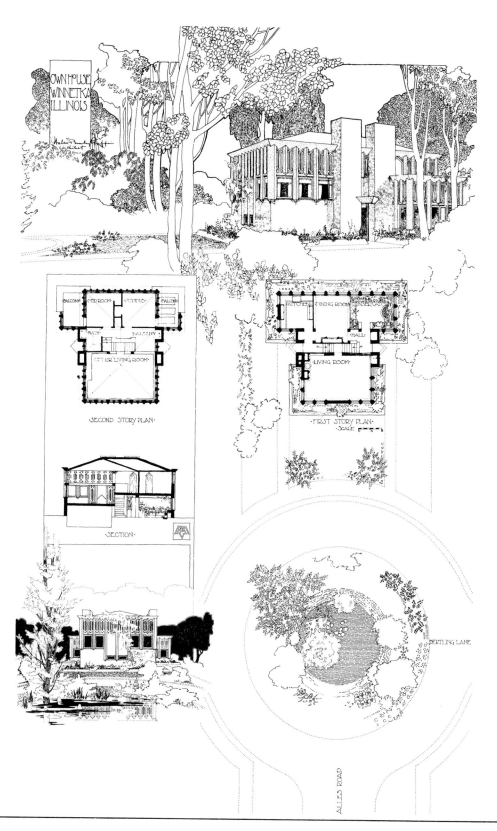

Walter Burley Griffin Residence
Winnetka, Illinois    1912
Ink on linen
37 × 22″ (94 × 56 cm)
Courtesy Northwestern University

156

J. G. Melson Residence
Mason City, Iowa    1912
Ink on linen
37 × 21½" (94 × 55 cm)
Courtesy Northwestern University

J. G. Melson Residence
Mason City, Iowa     1912
Photograph courtesy Thomas A. Heinz,
Architect
© Copyright Thomas A. Heinz 1979

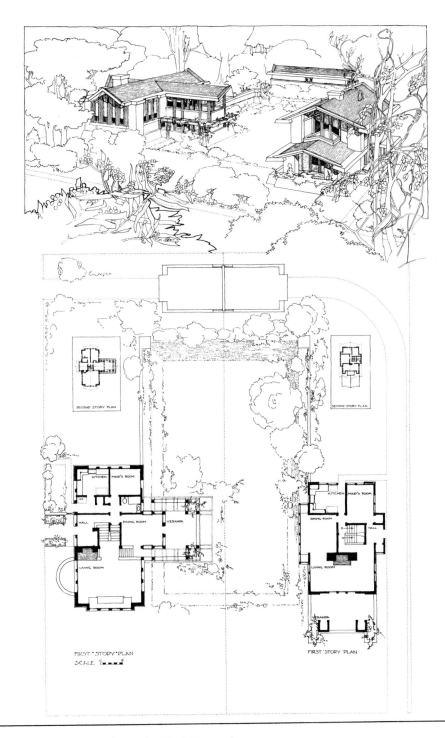

Two residences for Hurd Comstock
Evanston, Illinois    1912
Ink on linen
38½ × 22″ (98 × 56 cm)
Courtesy Northwestern University

Student Union Building
Lucknow University
Lucknow, India    1937
Pencil on paper
29⅞ × 24½" (76 × 62 cm)
Courtesy The Burnham Library, The Art
Institute of Milwaukee

# CLAUDE AND STARCK (1896-1929)

## LOUIS W. CLAUDE (1868-1951)
## EDWARD F. STARCK (1868-1947)

Based in Madison, Wisconsin, the architectural partnership and production of Claude and Starck is a fine example of the spread of the Prairie style throughout the smaller communities in the Midwest. Both Claude and Starck were born in Wisconsin in 1868. They received their architectural training both locally and in Milwaukee and Chicago. Louis Claude, in particular, followed a pattern of training very similar to that of Frank Lloyd Wright: first a few years at the University of Wisconsin studying engineering and working with Allan D. Conover and then on to Chicago to work for D. H. Burnham, Adler & Sullivan, among others. By 1896, Claude and Starck had both returned to Madison, and they began a partnership which would last until 1929. During these years, Claude and Starck were responsible for much of the Prairie style architecture in Madison and the surrounding area. This work included collaborations with other Prairie architects working in the area, including George Maher and Louis H. Sullivan.

Lincoln School
Monroe, Wisconsin    1915
Column capital, glazed terra cotta
32 × 29 × 29″ (81 × 74 × 74 cm)
Photographs from the Louis W. Claude
Collection, courtesy Mr. & Mrs. Gordon D. Orr, Jr.

162    George A. Lougee Residence
Madison, Wisconsin   1907
Photographs from the Louis W. Claude
Collection, courtesy Mr. & Mrs. Gordon D. Orr, Jr.

District No. 7 Grade School
Town of Madison, Wisconsin    1925
Photographs from the Louis W. Claude
Collection, courtesy Mr. & Mrs. Gordon D. Orr, Jr.

# RICHARD WALTER BOCK (1865-1949)

As a sculptor, Richard Bock was one of the independent craftsmen fundamental to the success of the Prairie style's harmonious unity of architecture, decoration, and environment. Although known primarily for his collaborations with Frank Lloyd Wright, Bock was responsible for sculptural ornament and detailing for several Prairie style buildings, as well as for independently commissioned sculpture which complemented the interior/exterior and the environmental setting. Born in Germany, Bock moved to Chicago with his family at an early age and was initially trained in his father's trade of woodworking and carving. Bock returned to Europe in 1888 to travel and to study, both in Berlin and at the École des Beaux Arts in Paris. Returning to Chicago in the early 1890s, Bock worked on various commissions, including sculptural decoration for some of the buildings at the 1893 World Colombian Exposition. When Bock was hired to work on Adler & Sullivan's Schiller Building of 1891-1892, he became acquainted with the young Frank Lloyd Wright. Bock's work for Wright began sometime between 1895 and 1898, with Bock's sculpture for the Oak Park studio. Their work together included the Dana Residence in Springfield, Illinois, of 1903; the Larkin Building in Buffalo, New York, of 1905; the Darwin D. Martin Residence in Buffalo, New York, of 1905; and the City National Bank in Mason City, Iowa, of 1909-1910. Bock's final commission for Wright was his work at Midway Gardens in Chicago in 1914. During and after his association with Wright, Bock worked with several other Prairie school architects, including Charles E. White, Jr., Robert C. Spencer, Jr., William Gray Purcell, and William Drummond. Most of these commissions were a single piece of sculpture or a fountain, such as the Skinner fountain which Bock designed in 1910. In the early 1920s, Bock's association with the Prairie movement ended, although he continued his career as an architectural sculptor and teacher at the universities of Oregon, Chicago, and California.

Larkin Company Administration Building
Buffalo, New York    circa 1904-1905
Exterior relief panel, full-sized plaster model
12¼ × 7" (31 × 18 cm)
Courtesy Greenville College
The Richard W. Bock Collection

The "Golf Bug," model for Riverside Golf
Club
North Riverside, Illinois    1930
Plaster
14 × 17 × 8″ (36 × 43 × 20 cm)
Courtesy Greenville College
The Richard W. Bock Collection

**166**　J. Fletcher Skinner Residence
Oak Park, Illinois　circa 1909-1910
Original photograph of fountain in situ
9 × 17¼" (23 × 44 cm)
Courtesy Greenville College
The Richard W. Bock Collection

J. Fletcher Skinner Residence
Oak Park, Illinois    circa 1909-1910
Head of Thor, model for fountain,
cast concrete with inlaid mosaic
15 × 6½ × 8½″ (38 × 17 × 22 cm)
Courtesy Greenville College
The Richard W. Bock Collection

# BENTLEY AND MERMAN

## PERCY DWIGHT BENTLEY (1885-1968)
## OTTO A. MERMAN (1890-1935)

Percy Dwight Bentley was born in La Crosse, Wisconsin, and studied architecture at Ohio Wesleyan University. After additional training at the Armour Institute in Chicago, Bentley apprenticed in the office of Wells E. Bennett in La Crosse. He started his own practice there about 1910 with the design of a residence for Edward C. Bartl, which showed the obvious influence of his exposure to Frank Lloyd Wright while attending school in Chicago.

Bentley soon hired Otto A. Merman as draftsman, and the firm maintained a strong design tie to the Prairie architects in Chicago with such projects as the Fix Residence of 1912 in Tomah, Wisconsin; the Chase Residence of 1913; the Felber Residence; the Emil T. Mueller Residence of 1915; and the 1912 Henry A. Salzer Residence (with furniture, carpeting, lighting fixtures, and color schemes by George M. Niedecken) in La Crosse.

The Emil T. Mueller Residence of 1914 was done in partnership with Charles A. Hauster of St. Paul, Minnesota, and was the last of Bentley's works in La Crosse. Otto A. Merman, Bentley's draftsman and later partner on several projects, assumed responsibility for the La Crosse office and continued, to a lesser degree, the pronounced Prairie school idiom of the earlier work with the design of the 1919 Trimble Residence in West Salem, Wisconsin; residences for Ed and Frank Schwalbe, Jr., in La Crosse in 1920; and the Emil Seitz Residence in Winona, Minnesota. After the Seitz Residence of 1922, few designs suggest a relationship to the Prairie style. Merman's death in 1935 and Bentley's move to Oregon in 1936 ended the influence of the Prairie school in La Crosse.

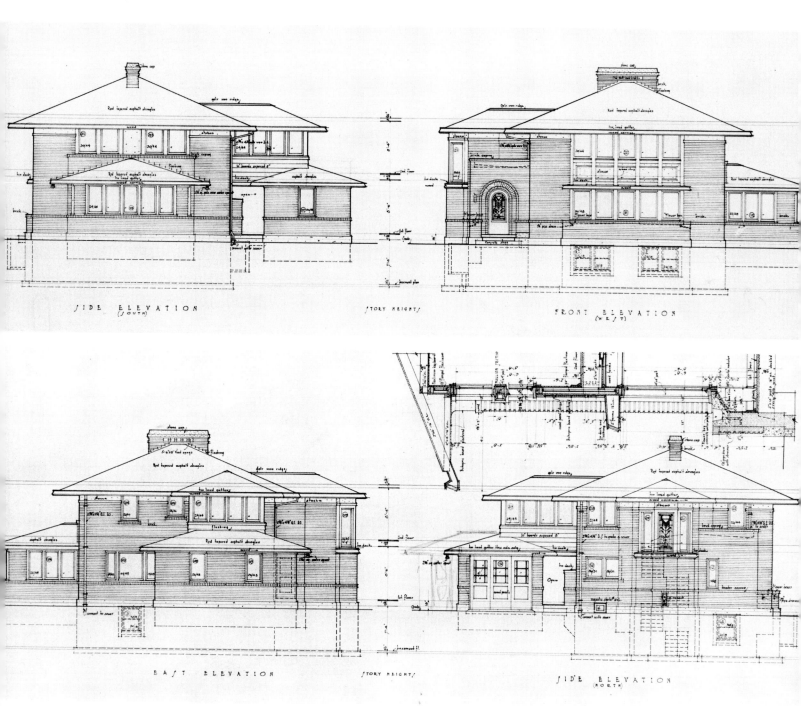

SIDE ELEVATION
(SOUTH)

STORY HEIGHTS

FRONT ELEVATION
(WEST)

EAST ELEVATION

STORY HEIGHTS

SIDE ELEVATION
(NORTH)

Frank Schwalbe, Jr., Residence
La Crosse, Wisconsin    1920
Ink on linen
18 × 36⅜" (46 × 92 cm)
Courtesy Peter Nelson and Sons

Frank Schwalbe, Jr., Residence
La Crosse, Wisconsin    1920
Ink on linen
18 × 36⅜" (46 × 92 cm)
Courtesy Peter Nelson and Sons

169

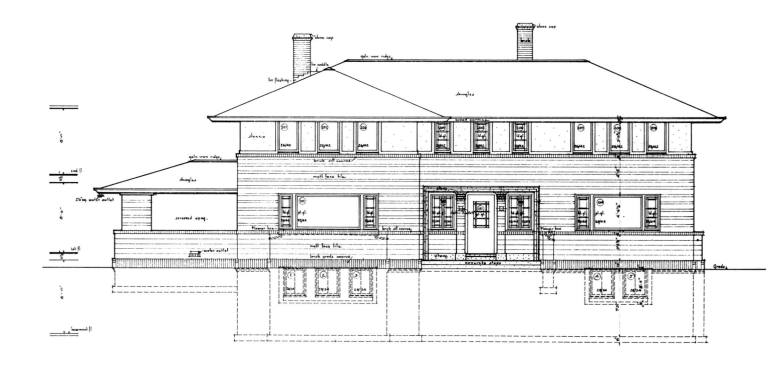

**170**   D. Trimble Residence
West Salem, Wisconsin    1919
Ink on linen
16⅝ × 30⅜" (42 × 77 cm)
Courtesy Peter Nelson and Sons

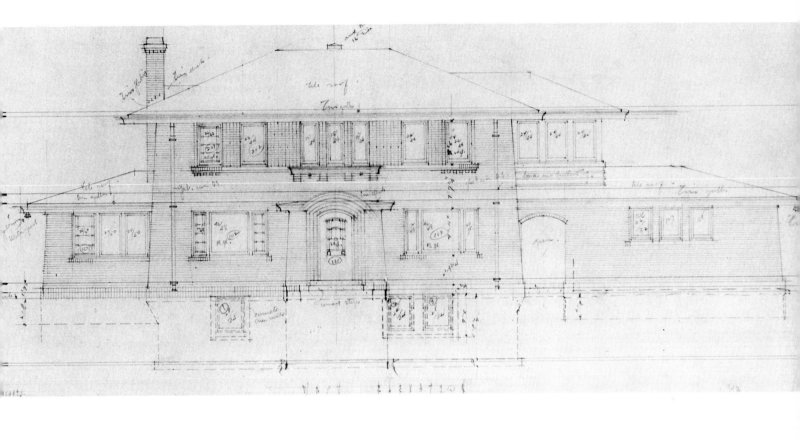

Emil Seitz Residence
Winona, Minnesota     1922
Pencil on tracing paper
11 × 23¾″ (28 × 60 cm)
Courtesy Peter Nelson and Sons

# GEORGE MANN NIEDECKEN (1878-1945)

Born in Milwaukee, Wisconsin, George Mann Niedecken received early training in art at Milwaukee art schools and at the Chicago Art Institute. In 1898, he left Chicago for further study in Europe, which included working with Alphonse Mucha in Paris, and he traveled extensively throughout France, Germany, Austria, and Italy. After returning to America in 1901, Niedecken's interest was expressed in design and interior decoration. In 1907, the Niedecken-Walbridge firm of "Interior Architects" was established, specializing in interior design, custom furniture design, mural painting, and art glass. Niedecken's Prairie style work lasted through the early 1920s and included collaboration with such Prairie school architects as Louis H. Sullivan, Frank Lloyd Wright, Spencer and Powers, Purcell and Elmslie, William Drummond, among others. Of Niedecken's most noted collaborations were those which he undertook with Frank Lloyd Wright, including the Robie and Coonley residences.

Wallpaper design    1902
Ink and watercolor on paper
5⅝ × 8¾" (14 × 22 cm)
Courtesy Mr. & Mrs. Robert L. Jacobson

173

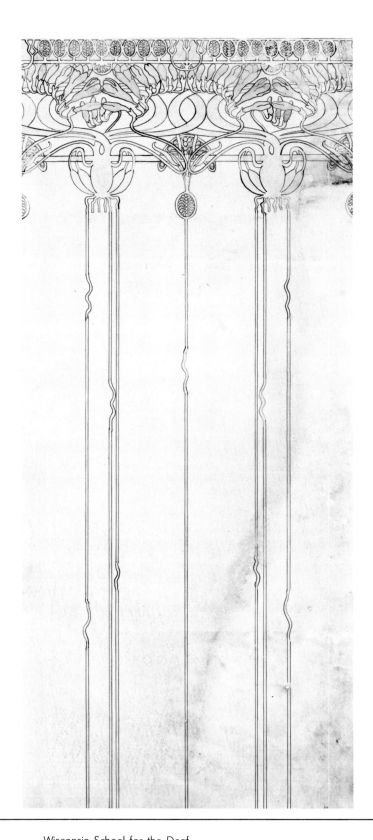

Wisconsin School for the Deaf
Delevan, Wisconsin    1902
Wall treatment, ink and
watercolor on paper
19⅞ × 8¾″ (51 × 22 cm)
Courtesy Mr. & Mrs. Robert L. Jacobson

Arts and crafts exhibition poster    no date
Litho print with pastels
28 × 20″ (71 × 51 cm)
Courtesy Mr. & Mrs. Robert L. Jacobson

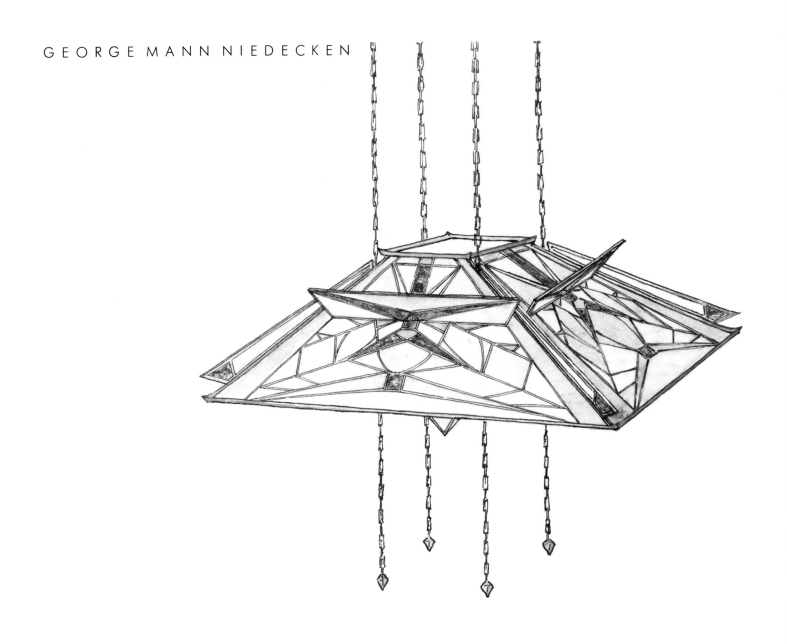

Possibly Susan Lawrence Dana Residence
Springfield, Illinois    1903
Art glass hanging light fixture, ink and
watercolor on paper
8 × 7½" (20 × 19 cm)
Courtesy Mr. & Mrs. Robert L. Jacobson

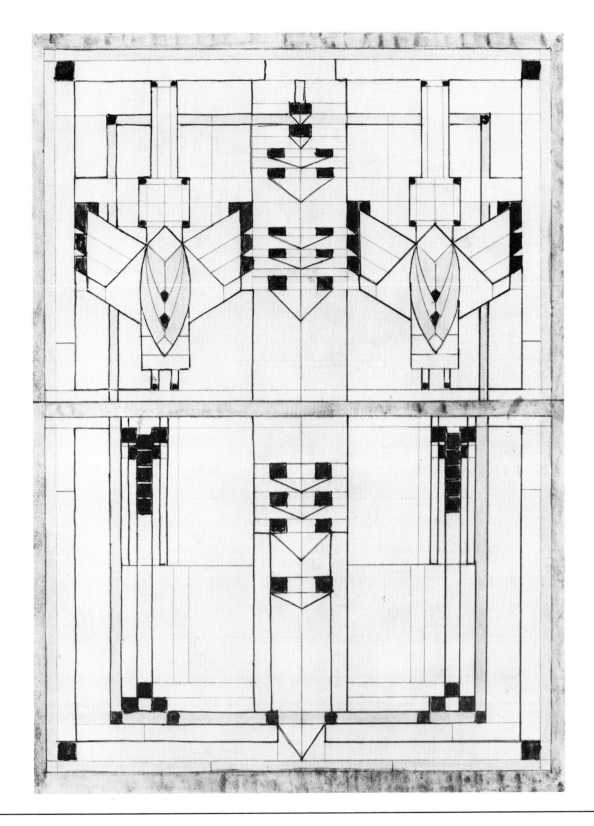

Design for art glass window
circa 1905-1910
Ink and watercolor on tracing paper
10⅜ × 7⅝" (26 × 19 cm)
Courtesy Mr. & Mrs. Robert L. Jacobson

178

Possible Niedecken design
Sedgwick S. Brinsmaid Residence
Des Moines, Iowa    circa 1902
Arthur Heun, Architect;
glass executed by O. Giannini
Wall sconce, wood with art glass shade
12½ × 6⅜ × 7¼" (32 × 16 × 18 cm)
Courtesy Thomas A. Heinz

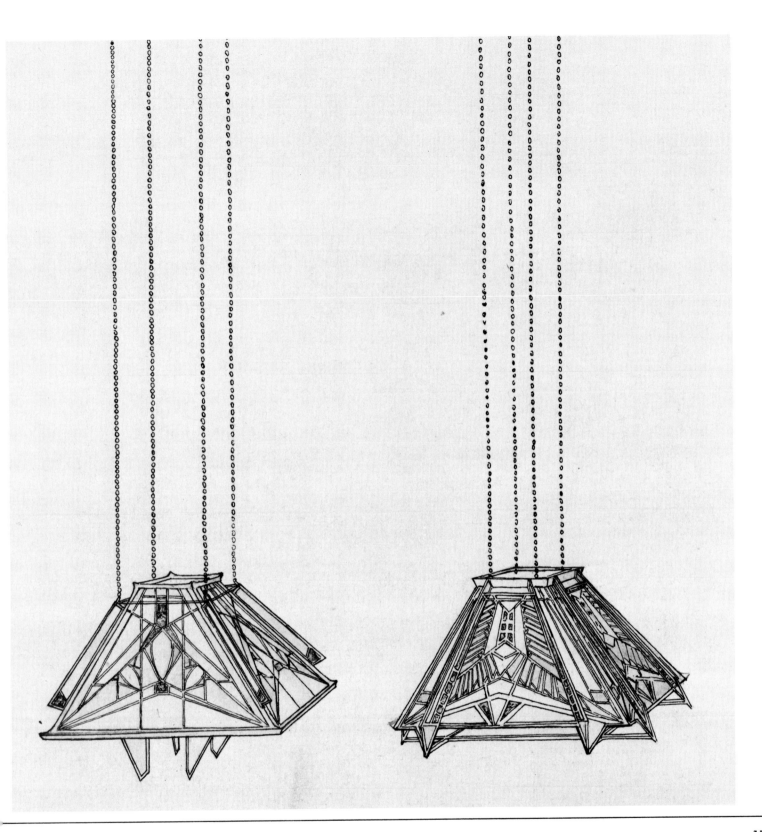

Lawrence Demmer Residence
Milwaukee, Wisconsin    1907-1916
Hanging art glass fixtures, ink and
watercolor on paper
9⅞ × 11″ (25 × 28 cm)
Courtesy Mr. & Mrs. Robert L. Jacobson

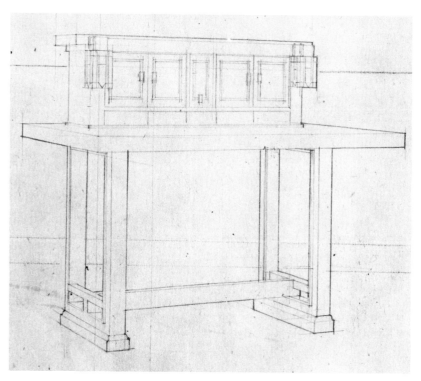

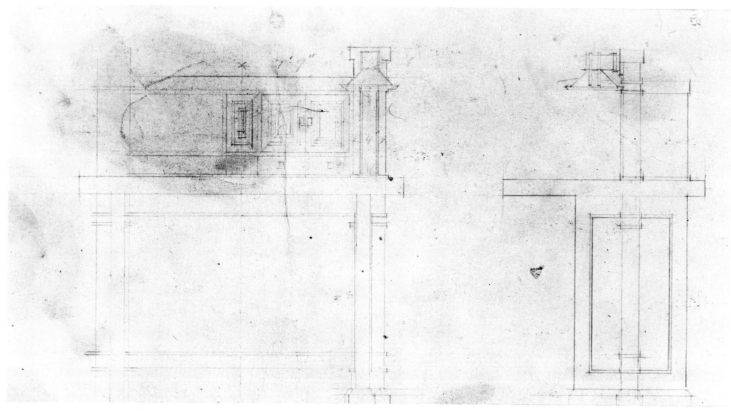

180

Desk for Warren Residence
circa 1907-1910
Pencil on kraft paper
11 × 15¾" (28 × 40 cm)
Courtesy Mr. & Mrs. Robert L. Jacobson

Desk for Frank Bressler
Milwaukee, Wisconsin    circa 1907-1910
Pencil on paper
12 × 16" (31 × 41 cm)
Courtesy Mr. & Mrs. Robert L. Jacobson

Design for music cabinet    1907
Pencil and watercolor on paper
7½ × 4½" (19 × 12 cm)
Courtesy Mr. & Mrs. Robert L. Jacobson

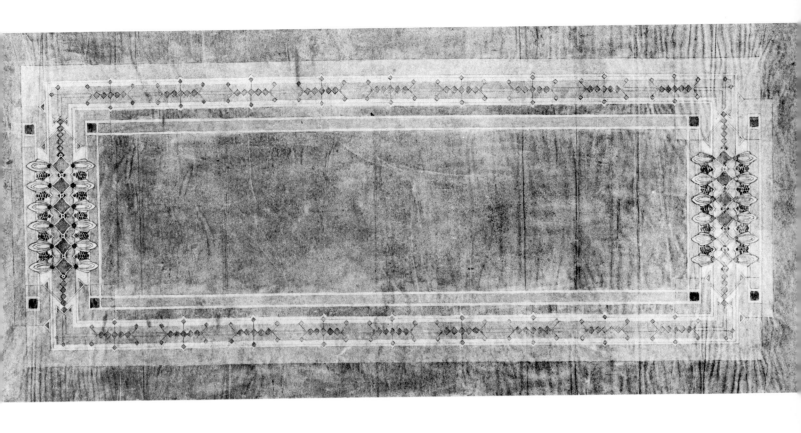

182     Edward Bradley Residence
Milwaukee, Wisconsin     circa 1910
Elmer Grey, architect
Rug design, pencil and
watercolor on tracing paper
9¾ × 24½" (24 × 62 cm)
Courtesy Mr. & Mrs. Robert L. Jacobson

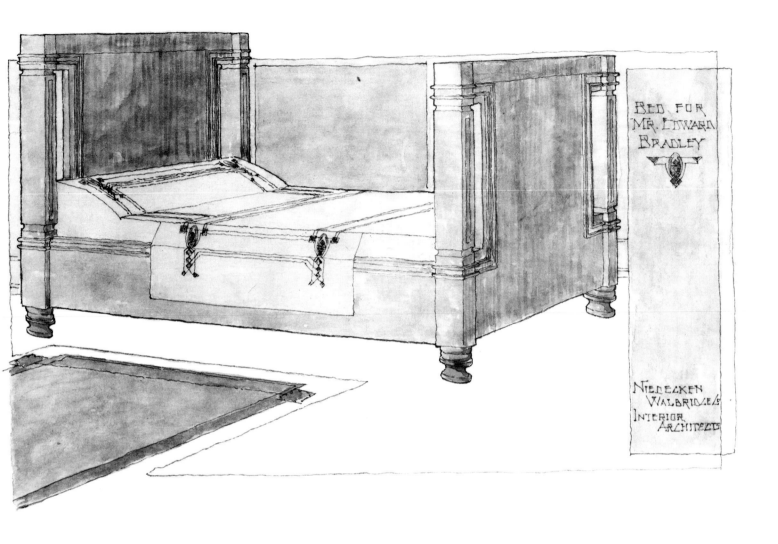

BED FOR
MR. EDWARD
BRADLEY

NIEDECKEN
WALBRIDGE/
INTERIOR
ARCHITECTS

Edward Bradley Residence
Milwaukee, Wisconsin    circa 1910
Elmer Grey, architect
Bed and linens, ink and
watercolor on tracing paper
7⅞ × 11" (20 × 28 cm)
Courtesy Mr. & Mrs. Robert L. Jacobson

184     Mr. F. A. Kieckhefer Residence
Design for library    1910
Ink and watercolor on paper
11⅝ × 26¾" (29 × 68 cm)
Courtesy Mr. & Mrs. Robert L. Jacobson

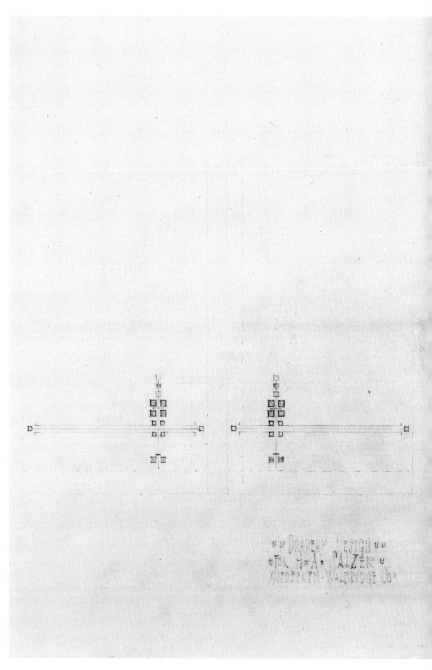

Milwaukee Athletic Club
Milwaukee, Wisconsin    1910-1920
Window treatment, pencil and
watercolor on tracing paper
15 × 10″ (38 × 25 cm)
Courtesy Mr. & Mrs. Robert L. Jacobson

Henry A. Salzer Residence
La Crosse, Wisconsin    1912
Percy Dwight Bentley, architect
Drapery design, pencil on tracing paper
11¾ × 9¼″ (30 × 24 cm)
Courtesy Mr. & Mrs. Robert L. Jacobson

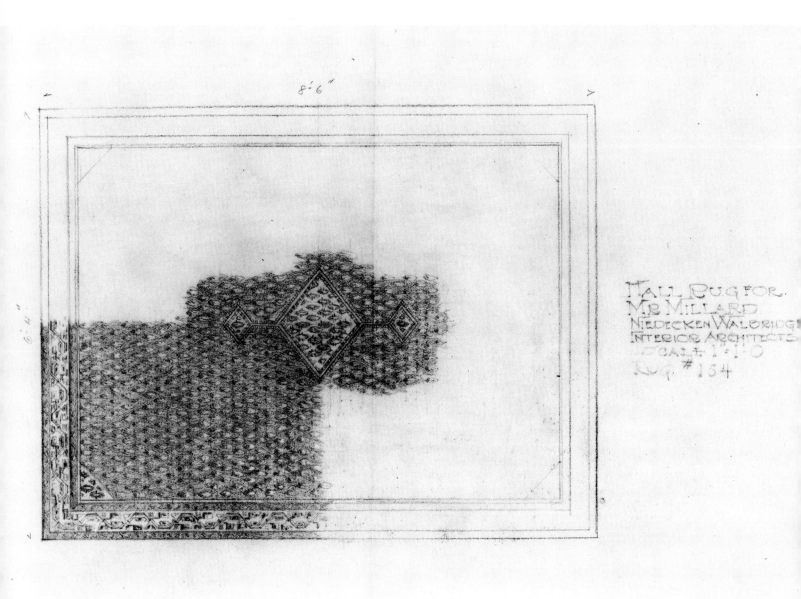

**186**   Hall rug for Millard Residence
Riverside, Illinois    1912
Colored pencil on tracing paper
11¾ × 16½" (30 × 42 cm)
Courtesy Mr. & Mrs. Robert L. Jacobson

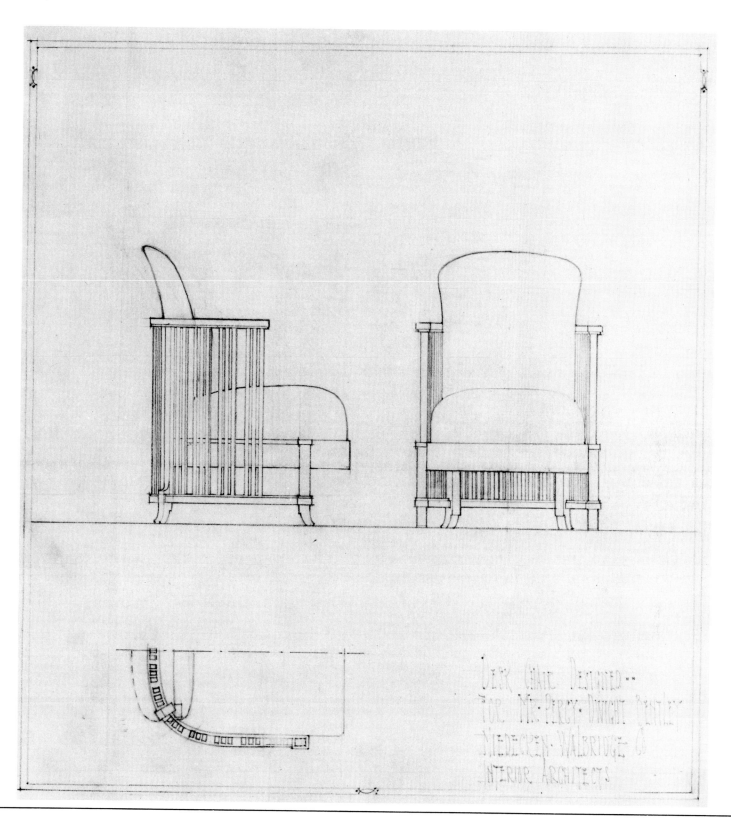

Desk chair for Percy Dwight Bentley
circa 1912
Pencil on paper
12½ × 11⅝" (32 × 30 cm)
Courtesy Mr. & Mrs. Robert L. Jacobson

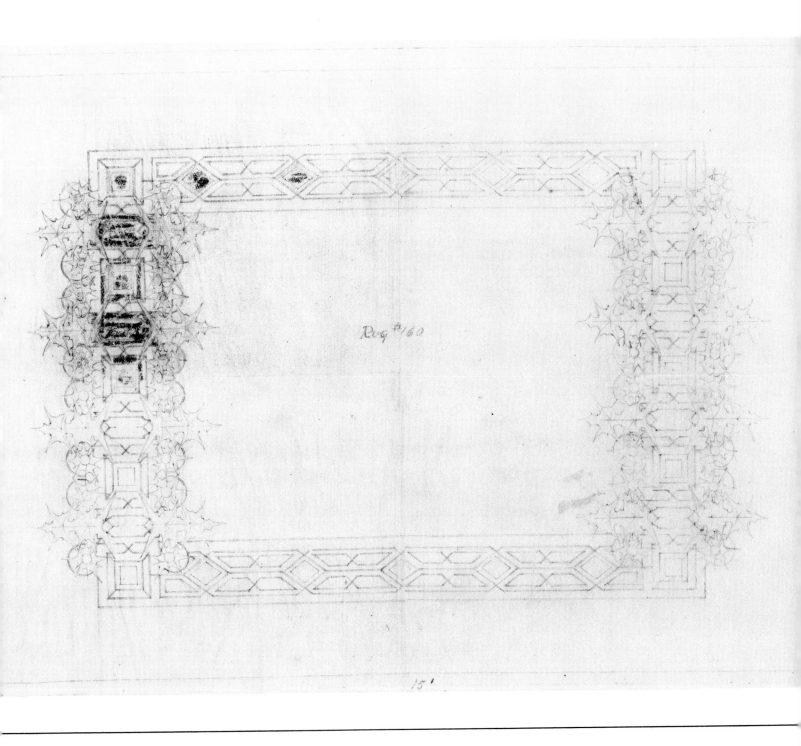

**188**   C. R. Carpenter Residence
Racine, Wisconsin    1912
Carpet design, pencil on tracing paper
11½ × 16" (29 × 41 cm)
Courtesy Mr. & Mrs. Robert L. Jacobson

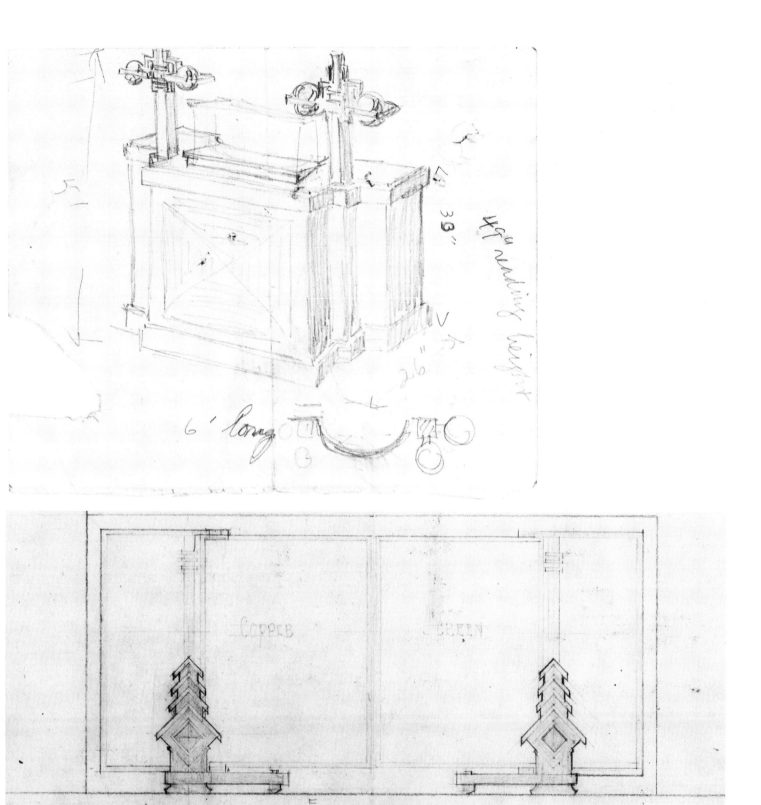

Milwaukee Downer College
Milwaukee, Wisconsin    1912-1913
Podium design, pencil on paper
5¼ × 6½" (13 × 17 cm)
Courtesy Mr. & Mrs. Robert L. Jacobson

Gustavus Babson Residence II
Oak Park, Illinois    1912-1913
Tallmadge and Watson, architects
Andiron design, pencil on tracing paper
11 × 11¾" (28 × 30 cm)
Courtesy Mr. & Mrs. Robert L. Jacobson

# GREENE AND GREENE (1894-1922)

## CHARLES SUMNER GREENE (1868-1957)
## HENRY MATHER GREENE (1870-1954)

Born in Ohio, the Greene brothers were introduced to the ideas and fundamentals of the Arts and Crafts movement at Calvin Woodward's Manual Training High School in St. Louis and to architecture at MIT. After a visit to Pasadena in 1893, the brothers decided to settle in Southern California. Here they remained, creating a unique style of architecture reflecting the integration of Oriental, English and Swiss influences with the native mission tradition of the Southwest. Their most innovative work—commissions executed during the first decade of the century—shows an immediate kinship with contemporary developments in the Midwest. Foremost among their concerns was an extremely high degree of craftsmanship, combined with a desire for a total unity of architecture and environment, interior and exterior space, and the building and its furnishings. Their extremely high quality of craftsmanship can be seen both in the individualized and carefully detailed construction of their houses as well as in the furnishings, which included custom-designed furniture, glass, and rugs.

Adelaide M. Tichenor Residence
Long Beach, California    1904
Desk, ash
50½ × 31 × 16" (128 × 79 × 41 cm)
Courtesy Randall L. Makinson

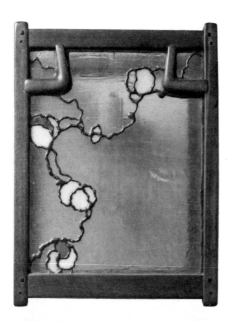

James A. Culbertson Residence
Pasadena, California     1906
Interior wall lantern, mahogany and
art glass
14½ × 10¾ × 7¼" (37 × 27 × 18 cm)
Courtesy Ronald R. Chitwood

Adelaide M. Tichenor Residence
Long Beach, California     1904
Bedroom windows (2), leaded stained
art glass with lead overlay
27¾ × 18" (70 × 46 cm) each
Courtesy Ronald R. Chitwood

192    Henry M. Robinson Residence
Pasadena, California    1905
Den table lamp, oak and fabric
22 × 20 × 20″ (56 × 51 × 51 cm)
Courtesy The Gamble House,
The University of Southern California, and
The City of Pasadena

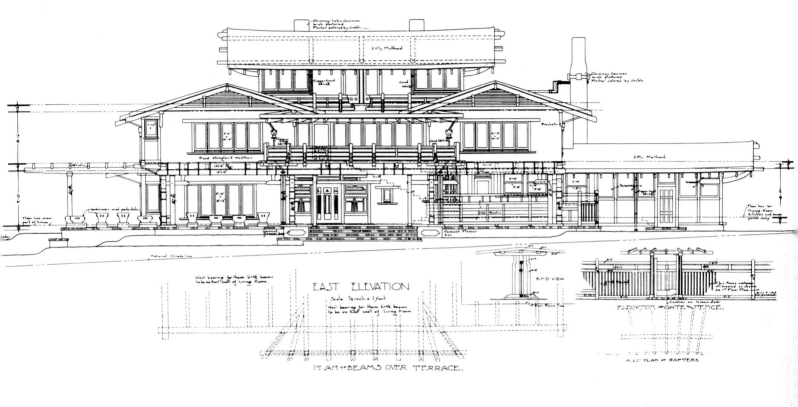

RESIDENCE. FOR FREEMAN A. FORD E. SQ AT PASADENA. CAL.

GREENE AND GREENE. ARCH'TS 215 BOSTON BLD'G PASADENA. CAL.

SHEET No 4                                                    MAY 13th '07.

EAST ELEVATION

PLAN OF BEAMS OVER TERRACE.

ELEVATION OF GATE & FENCE.

Freeman A. Ford Residence
Pasadena, California      1907
Ink on linen
22 × 35" (56 × 89 cm) each
Courtesy Greene and Greene Library,
The Gamble House,
University of Southern California

194    Robert R. Blacker Residence
Pasadena, California    1907
Courtesy Municipal Arts Department, City
of Los Angeles, and The Gamble House,
University of Southern California

Robert R. Blacker Residence
Pasadena, California    1907
Courtesy Municipal Arts Department, City
of Los Angeles, and The Gamble House,
University of Southern California

196    David B. Gamble Residence
Pasadena, California    1908
Courtesy The Gamble House, University of
Southern California, and The City of
Pasadena

David B. Gamble Residence
Pasadena, California    1908
Study for carpet for living room,
watercolor on paper
15½ × 19½" (39 × 50 cm)
Photograph courtesy The Gamble House,
University of Southern California, and The
City of Pasadena

David B. Gamble Residence
Pasadena, California    1908
Courtesy The Gamble House, University of
Southern California, and The City of
Pasadena

# LLOYD WRIGHT (1890-1978)

One of the two architect sons of Frank Lloyd Wright, Lloyd Wright was raised in the Oak Park, Illinois, studio of his father. Like his father, he began studying engineering at the University of Wisconsin, but ended his formal education at the request of his father to assist, along with Taylor Wolley, in the preparation of the drawings for the Wasmuth Portfolio of 1910.

After approximately three months in Europe working on the drawings, Lloyd Wright returned to the United States and spent a short period in the Boston office of Olmsted & Olmsted before moving to the West Coast to work on plans for Balboa Park in San Diego for that firm. When the Olmsted firm withdrew from the project, he began working for Irving Gill, Architect, in San Diego.

Lloyd Wright's earliest design was a Prairie style residence for the Midwest dated 1907, but his own style of architecture did not begin to emerge until 1926 with the designs for the Fairfax Theater and the Sowden Residence in Los Angeles. Many of his residential studies during this time were worked in textured concrete block, which his father expanded upon and developed into "knit block" construction.

Lloyd Wright maintained his practice in architecture, landscape design, and planning in Los Angeles. His commissions ranged from residential designs to planning the city of Torrance, California, and he even projected plans for Los Angeles and the "City of the Future." Though possibly overshadowed by his famous father, his search for "his own architecture" was never stifled. It can be seen in the wide scope of design he maintained in his practice, although it was not until a small chapel, Wayfarer's Chapel of 1946, was completed that his work gained greater public attention.

198

Middle West Residence
Oak Park, Illinois    1907
Ink on board
12½ × 23" (32 × 58 cm)
Courtesy Lloyd Wright, Architect

200    Fairfax Theatre
Los Angeles, California    1926
Pencil and paint on paper
20 × 21″ (51 × 53 cm)
Courtesy Lloyd Wright, Architect

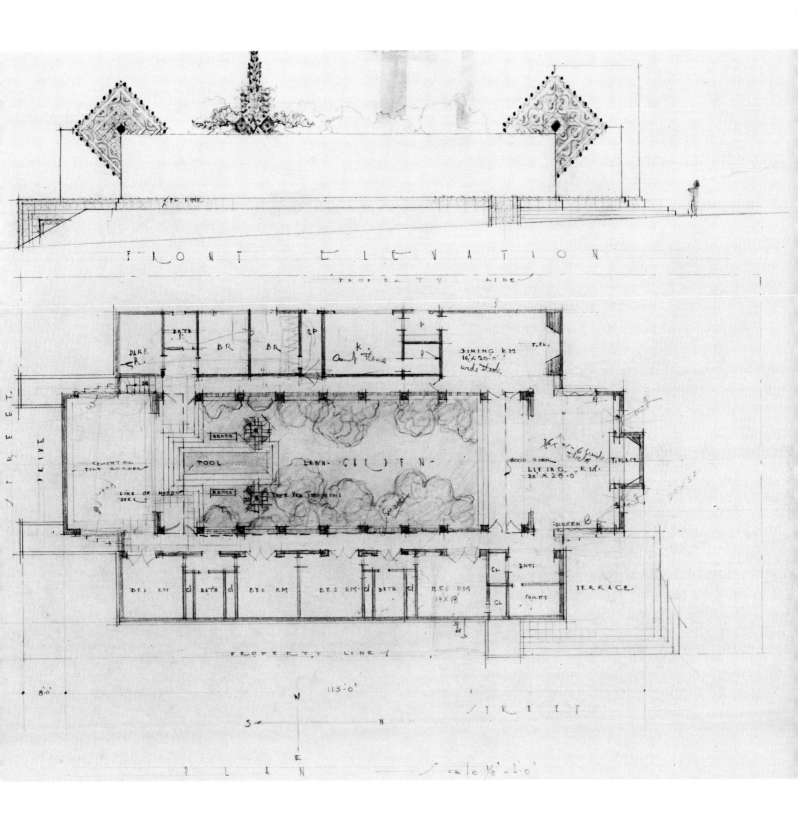

Sowden Residence, First Scheme
Los Angeles, California     1926
Pencil on paper
21 × 23½" (53 × 60 cm)
Courtesy Lloyd Wright, Architect

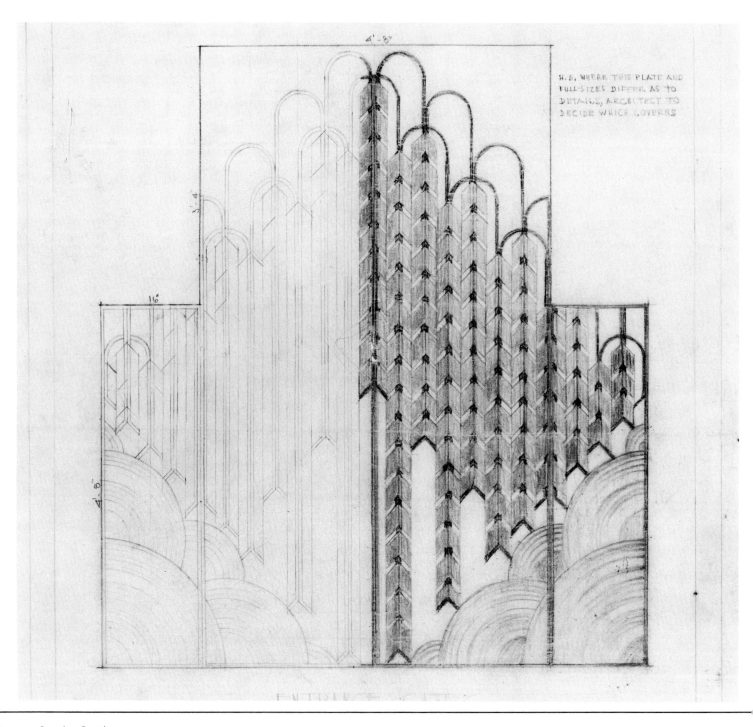

**202**  Sowden Residence
Los Angeles, California      1926
Entrance gate, pencil on paper
22 × 21″ (56 × 53 cm)
Courtesy Lloyd Wright, Architect

Sowden Residence, Second Scheme
Los Angeles, California    1926
Courtesy Lloyd Wright, Architect

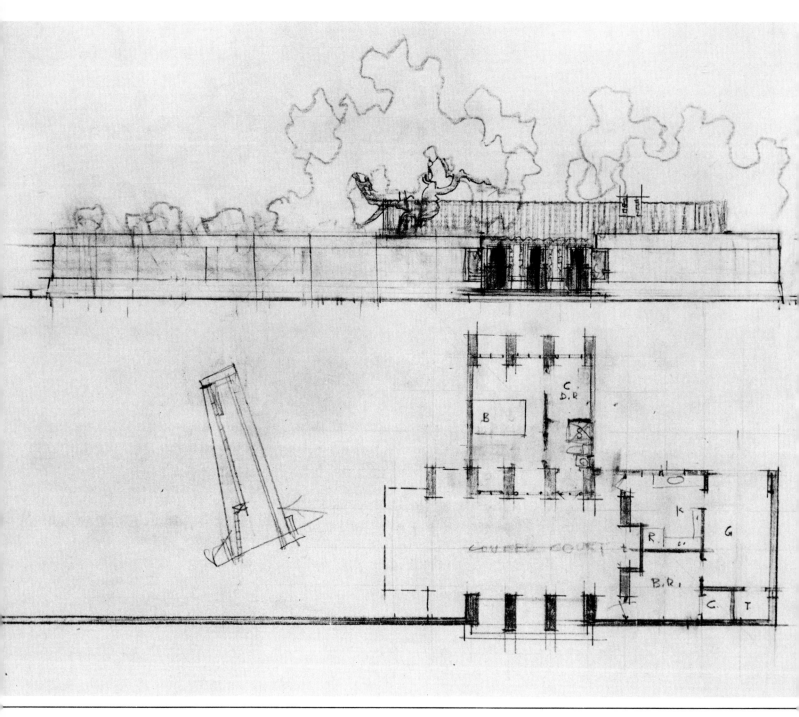

**204** Residential project
Chevy Chase, California    1926
Pencil on paper
20 × 32″ (51 × 81 cm)
Courtesy Lloyd Wright, Architect

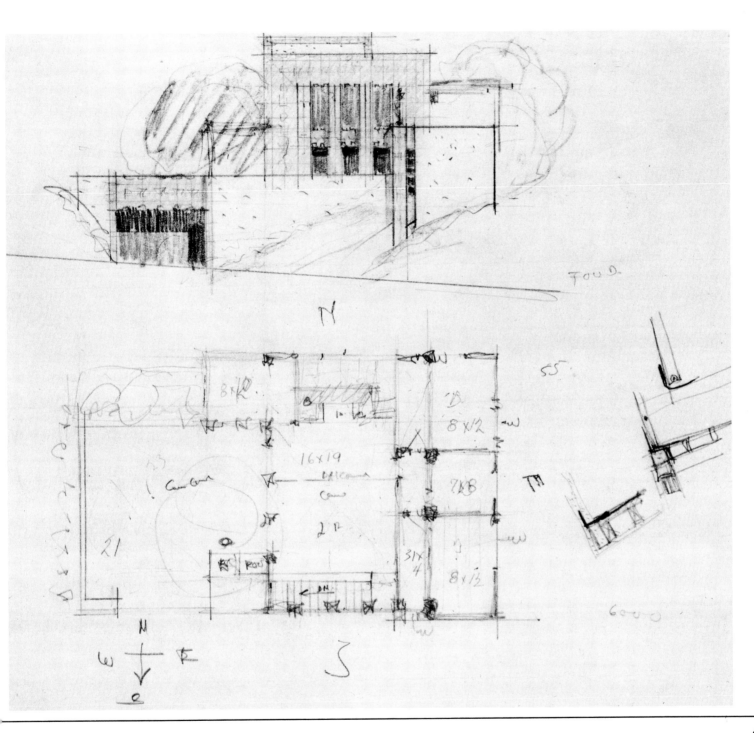

Will Connell Residence
Los Angeles, California    1927
Pencil on paper
15¾ × 14" (40 × 36 cm)
Courtesy Lloyd Wright, Architect

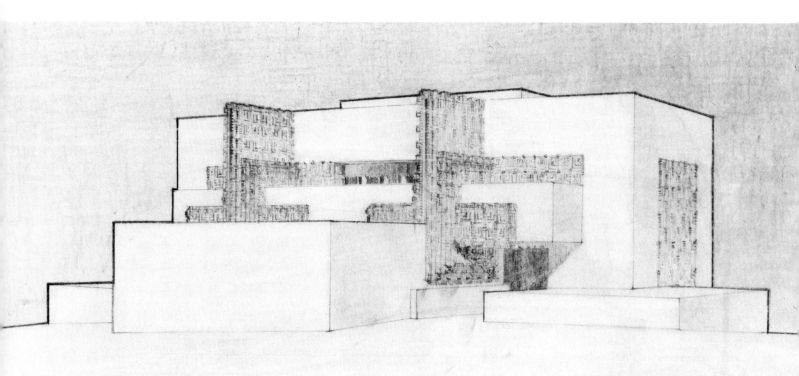

**206**   Lloyd Wright Residence and Studio
Los Angeles, California   1927
Pencil and charcoal on paper
13½ × 25½" (34 × 65 cm)
Courtesy Lloyd Wright, Architect

Lloyd Wright Residence and Studio
Los Angeles, California    1927
Early photograph
Courtesy Lloyd Wright, Architect

**208**   Desert Dune Berm House   1927
Pencil on paper
14 × 21″ (36 × 53 cm)
Courtesy Lloyd Wright, Architect

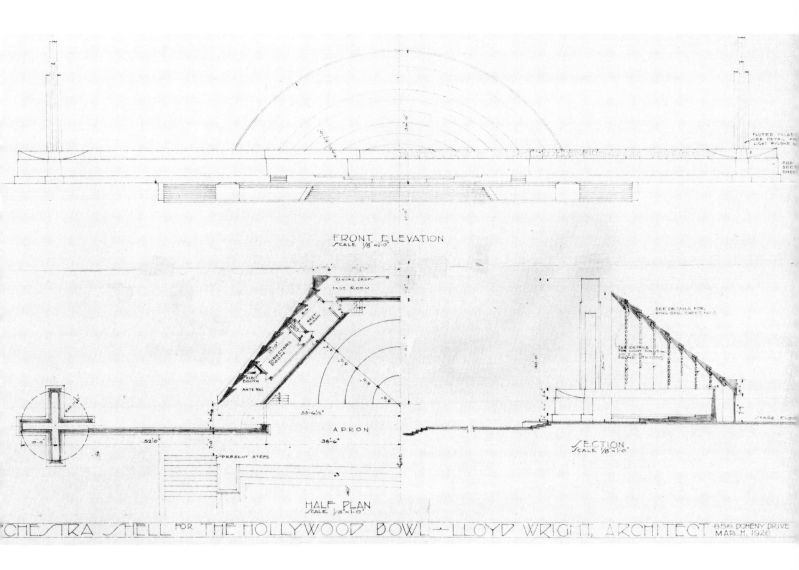

FRONT ELEVATION
SCALE 1/8=1'-0"

HALF PLAN
SCALE 1/8=1'-0"

SECTION
SCALE 1/8=1'-0"

CHESTRA SHELL FOR THE HOLLYWOOD BOWL — LLOYD WRIGHT, ARCHITECT 858 DOHENY DRIVE
MARCH, 1928

Second Shell for Hollywood Bowl
Hollywood, California      1928
Pencil on print paper
18¾ × 31¾" (48 × 81 cm)
Courtesy Lloyd Wright, Architect

210

Catholic Cathedral project
Los Angeles, California    1931
Pencil and tempera on paper
29 × 39″ (74 × 99 cm)
Courtesy Lloyd Wright, Architect

Drive-In Open Air Market and
Restaurant Project
Arcadia and Monrovia, California (?)
1931
Photograph courtesy Lloyd Wright

212    Phil Hanna Residence
       Chevy Chase, California    1933
       Pencil and tempera on paper
       11 × 18" (28 × 46 cm)
       Courtesy Lloyd Wright, Architect

Theta Chi Fraternity House
University of California
Los Angeles, California    1936
Tempera and charcoal on board
16½ × 21½" (42 × 55 cm)
Courtesy Lloyd Wright, Architect

214 Francis Blalock Residence
Los Angeles, California    1938
Pencil and tempera on paper
16 × 19″ (41 × 48 cm)
Courtesy Lloyd Wright, Architect

Harold Swann Residence
Santa Barbara, California    1940
Pencil on paper
16 × 28″ (41 × 71 cm)
Courtesy Lloyd Wright, Architect

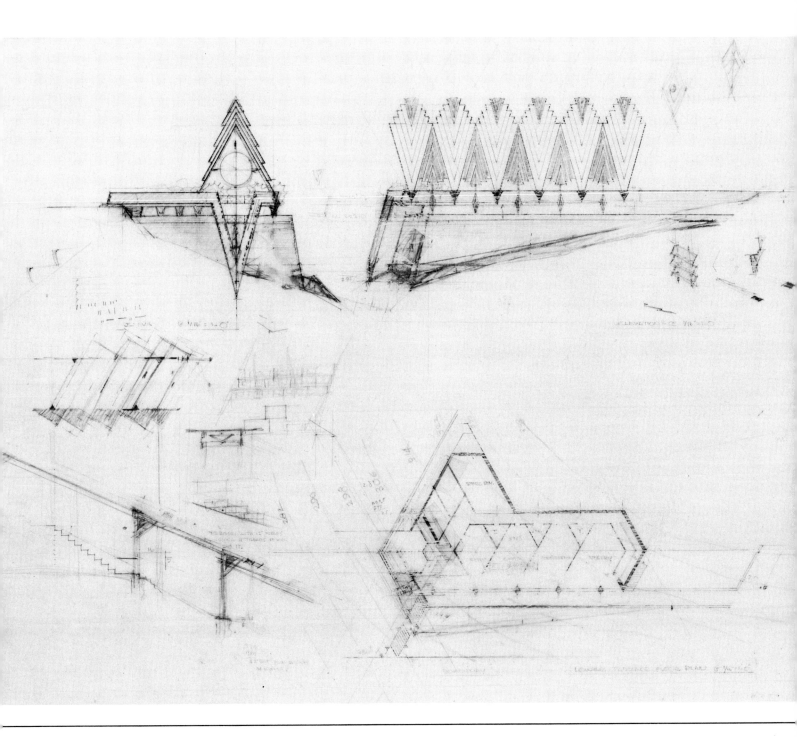

Swedenborg Memorial Chapel
El Cerrito, California     1955
Pencil on paper
22 × 28½″ (56 × 72 cm)
Courtesy Lloyd Wright, Architect

216      Bowler Residence
          Palos Verdes, California    1963
          Courtesy Lloyd Wright, Architect

University of California, Santa Barbara
Student Housing
La Jolla, California    1964
Photograph courtesy Lloyd Wright,
Architect

# BRUCE GOFF (BORN 1904)

Bruce Goff was born near Tulsa, Oklahoma, on the same day, June 8, as Frank Lloyd Wright, although thirty-seven years later. Their paths were to cross frequently, and their life patterns were not dissimilar.

Goff apprenticed, beginning at age twelve in the firm of Rush, Endicott & Rush in Tulsa. His first introduction to Wright came in 1916, when Rush showed him the March 1908 issue of *Architectural Record* after Goff designed a house similar to those of Wright.

During his early professional career, Goff practiced much in the manner of Frank Lloyd Wright, but his constant awareness of the experiments and growth of others, such as Eric Mendelsohn, Alfonso Iannelli, Gustav Klimt—architects, sculptors, artists, and musicians—added to the unique development of his own work.

Goff became a partner of Rush, Endicott & Rush in 1928, but the Great Depression a year later severely limited building and construction. In 1934 Goff relocated in Chicago where he taught a class at the Chicago Academy of Fine Arts. The Academy was headed by Mrs. Ford for whom he designed one of his most well-known houses in 1949. Goff's time as head of the design department for Libbey-Owens-Ford Glass Company and the one summer he spent with a Tulsa stone company helped develop his sensitivity to materials.

In 1941 Goff joined the Navy and designed a group of buildings in the Aleutians, followed by the chapel at Camp Park, California. Following the war years, he was chairman of the School of Architecture at the University of Oklahoma and in 1958 established his office in Wright's Price Tower in Bartlesville, Oklahoma, later moving to Kansas City. Since late 1970, he has practiced from his studio in Tyler, Texas.

Goff's architectural designs utilize uncommon or new materials, define new forms, and create new spaces. His work constantly attracts attention—not always favorable and not unlike reactions to the work of Wright in 1893.

Page Warehouse
Tulsa, Oklahoma    1927
Courtesy Bruce Goff, Architect

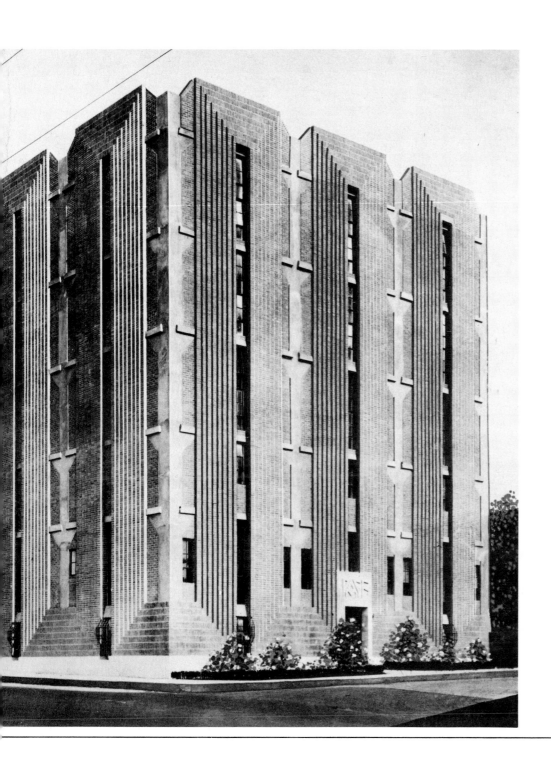

220    Ford Residence
Aurora, Illinois    1949
Courtesy Bruce Goff, Architect

Crystal Chapel
University of Oklahoma
Norman, Oklahoma     1949
Colored pencil on tracing paper
33 × 23½" (84 × 60 cm)
Courtesy Bruce Goff, Architect

222  Stuhlmann Residence
Baltimore, Maryland    1951
Colored pencil on tracing paper
20¾ × 36¼" (53 × 92 cm)
Courtesy Bruce Goff, Architect

Bavinger Residence
Norman, Oklahoma    1950
Courtesy Bruce Goff, Architect

224    Dewlen Residence
       Amarillo, Texas    1956
       Colored pencil on paper
       23 × 34″ (58 × 86 cm)
       Courtesy Bruce Goff, Architect

Joe Price Studio, Scheme 1
Starview Farm, Bartlesville,
Oklahoma    1955
Colored pencil on tracing paper
28 × 44″ (71 × 112 cm)
Courtesy Bruce Goff, Architect

Garvey Residence II
Urbana, Illinois    no date
Colored pencil on paper
23½ × 41½″ (58 × 105 cm)
Courtesy Bruce Goff, Architect

226  Black Bear Motor Lodge for Craeger Enterprises
Jackson Hole, Wyoming   1961
Black line print on gold paper
28¼ × 44" (72 × 112 cm)
Courtesy Bruce Goff, Architect

Hyde Residence
Kansas City, Kansas    1965
Courtesy Bruce Goff, Architect

# EDGAR A. TAFEL (BORN 1912)

Edgar A. Tafel was born and raised in New York. Following graduation from high school, he enrolled in architecture at New York University for one year. He then applied to the Taliesin Fellowship and was accepted by Frank Lloyd Wright as an apprentice. He joined the fellowship in the fall of 1932.

During his time with the Taliesin Fellowship, Tafel worked in the drafting room and field supervised construction of Edgar J. Kaufmann's Residence, "Fallingwater," in 1935, Herbert Jacobs' first residence designed by Frank Lloyd Wright in 1936, the S. C. Johnson & Son Administration Building of 1936, as well as Johnson's Residence, "Wingspread," in 1937. He also supervised the construction in 1939 of the Lloyd Lewis Residence and the Bernard Schwartz Residence, which is also called the *"Life* Magazine House" because it was featured in the magazine.

Edgar Tafel left the Taliesin Fellowship in the fall of 1941, spending about a year in architectural offices in Chicago, and then in 1942 he moved to Flagstaff, Arizona, where he was employed by a Detroit firm as a construction engineer. During World War II he was stationed in India with the armed forces, and after he was discharged in 1946, he returned to his native New York to begin his own practice of architecture. His firm has an active practice in planning and designing colleges, schools, churches, synagogues, social service facilities, as well as museums and residences. Under the auspices of the United States Information Service, he has lectured on organic architecture and his years of apprenticeship under Frank Lloyd Wright in England, Greece, India, Israel, Mexico and The Netherlands. In 1979 he published a book entitled *Apprentice to Genius.*

Parish House
First Presbyterian Church
New York, New York    1959
Courtesy Edgar A. Tafel, Architect

# ARTHUR A. CARRARA (BORN 1914)

Arthur A. Carrara was born in Chicago in 1914. He received his architectural education at the University of Illinois and began his apprenticeship under John Van Bergen, who had worked in the Oak Park studio of Frank Lloyd Wright and in the office of Walter Burley Griffin.

Carrara's own practice has been as prolific as that of his inspirational mentors'—chiefly Frank Lloyd Wright. Following World War II, Carrara held the principal responsibility for the plan of rebuilding the city of Manila. His concept for the Cafe Borranical in Melbourne, Australia, of 1945, introduced hydraulics into building design. And his designs for residences, industrial buildings, churches, furniture, lighting fixtures, and children's toys (such as Magnet Master, commissioned by the Walker Art Center in 1947) are fresh and innovative.

With offices in Buffalo and Chicago, Carrara's main studio and home are located in the wooded moraines of Wisconsin, near Whitewater. Tebah I and II, as he named his home and studio, provide living and work spaces, as well as being experimental structures for design ideas.

Tebah I incorporates a 50-foot (1-meter) single mold fiberglass skylight over a seasonally adaptive roof structure. The house and studio reflect total architectural control as practiced by the earlier Prairie school architects, with lighting fixtures, furniture, and decorative arts totally integral and designed by the architect.

Carrara's earlier designs for the Magnet Master toy led to studies in the use of magnetics in building construction. The experimental skylight in Tebah I (begun in 1962 and constantly changing) provided the basis for use of the material in the Graphic Controls Corporation's recently completed building in Mexico, and the prototype keel chair and table were the design studies for the structure of the Dyett Residence four years later in 1963.

To ensure presentation of his philosophy, Carrara has designed exhibitions of his work which were presented at the Walker Art Center, the Milwaukee Art Center, and the Munson-Williams-Proctor Institute. In the tradition of the Prairie school architects, he designed the presentation catalogue accompanying the exhibitions.

Edward W. Kuhn Residence
Chicago, Illinois    1952
Pencil on tracing paper
10¼ × 15¼" (26 × 39 cm)
Courtesy Arthur A. Carrara, Architect

232    Reno J. Carrara Residence
Whitewater, Wisconsin   1954
Pencil on paper
7½ × 14" (19 × 36 cm)
Courtesy Arthur A. Carrara, Architect

Reno J. Carrara Residence
Whitewater, Wisconsin    1954
Courtesy Arthur A. Carrara, Architect

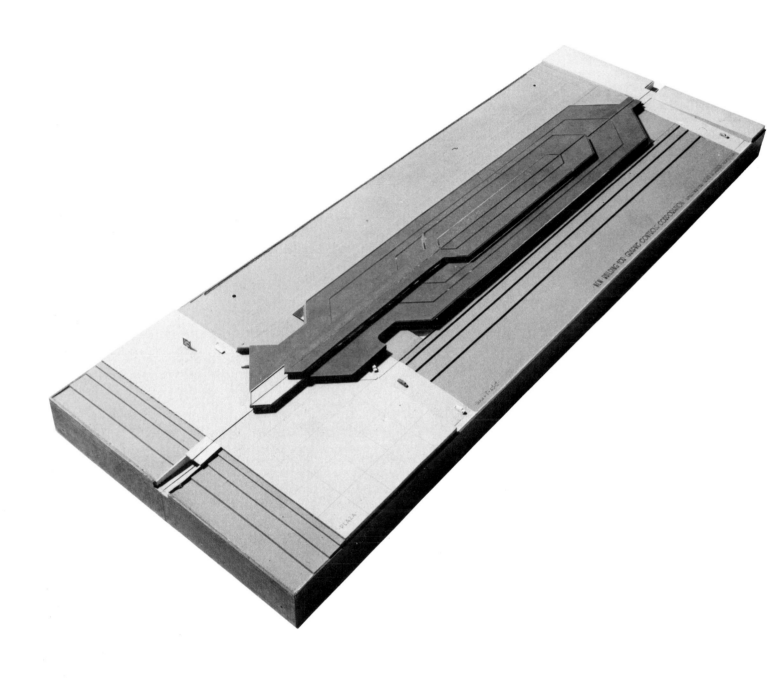

234    Graphic Controls Corporation
Buffalo, New York    1961
Courtesy Arthur A. Carrara, Architect

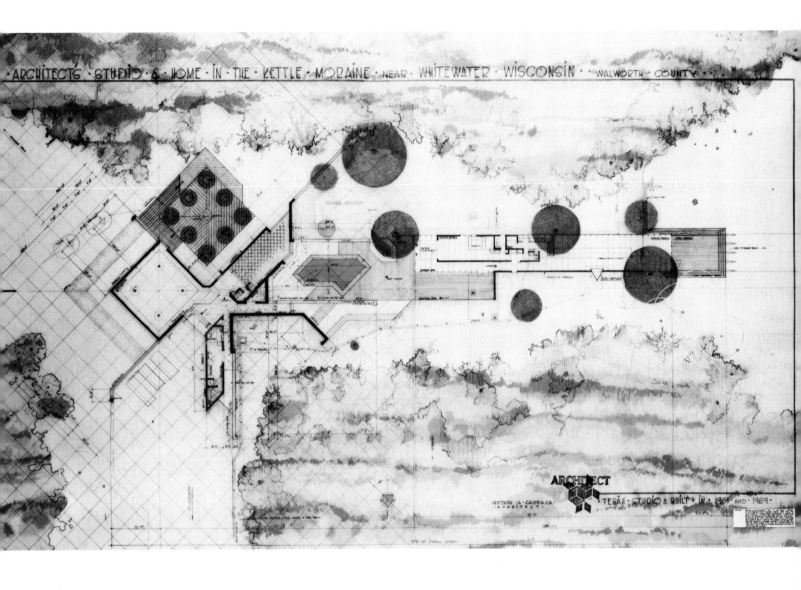

"Tebah I and II,"
Arthur A. Carrara Studio and Home
Whitewater, Wisconsin    1961 and 1969
Pen, ink, and silk on mylar
30 × 50" (76 × 127 cm)
Courtesy Arthur A. Carrara, Architect

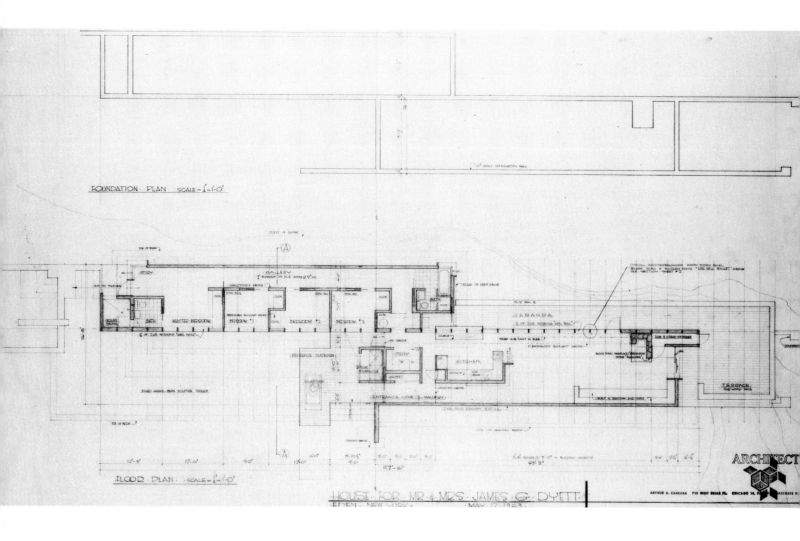

236   James G. Dyett Residence
Eden, New York    1963
Pencil on paper
24⅛ × 42½″ (61 × 108 cm)
Courtesy Arthur A. Carrara, Architect

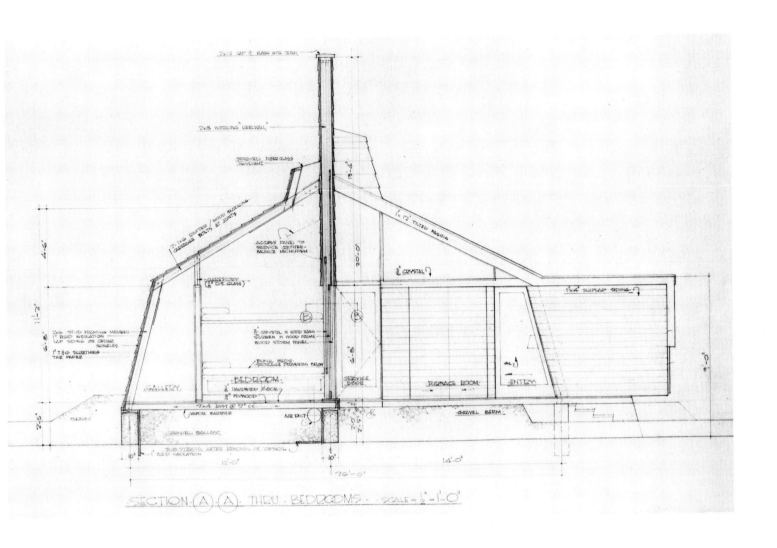

SECTION ·(A)·(A)· THRU · BEDROOMS · SCALE = ½" = 1'-0"

James G. Dyett Residence
Eden, New York    1963
Pencil on paper
22¼ × 42½" (56 × 108 cm)
Courtesy Arthur A. Carrara, Architect

238

Yoke Lamp    1960
Plywood, plastic tubing, and concrete
48 × 7½ × 7½" (122 × 19 × 19 cm)
Courtesy Arthur A. Carrara, Architect

Keel chair and table    1959
Stapled fir plywood
35¾ × 24 × 26 (90 × 61 × 66 cm);
16 × 36 × 41″ (41 × 91 × 104 cm)
Courtesy Arthur A. Carrara, Architect

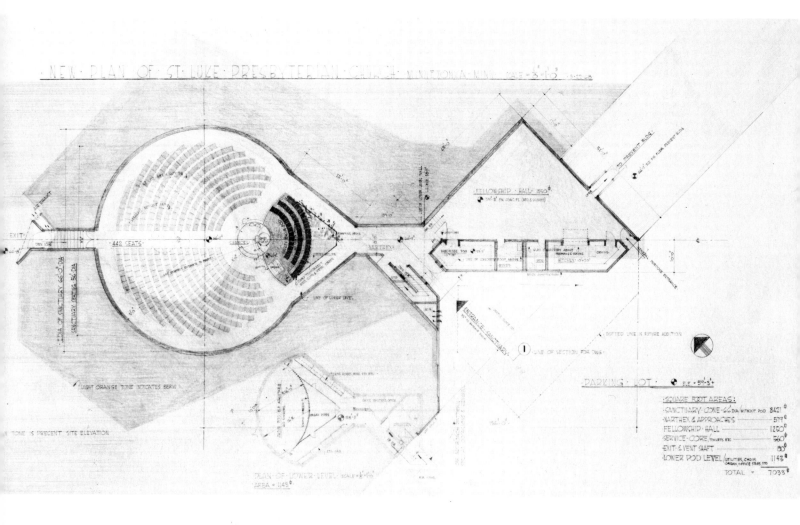

240    St. Luke Presbyterian Church
       Minnetonka, Minnesota    1968
       Plan, colored pencil on paper
       Courtesy Arthur A. Carrara, Architect

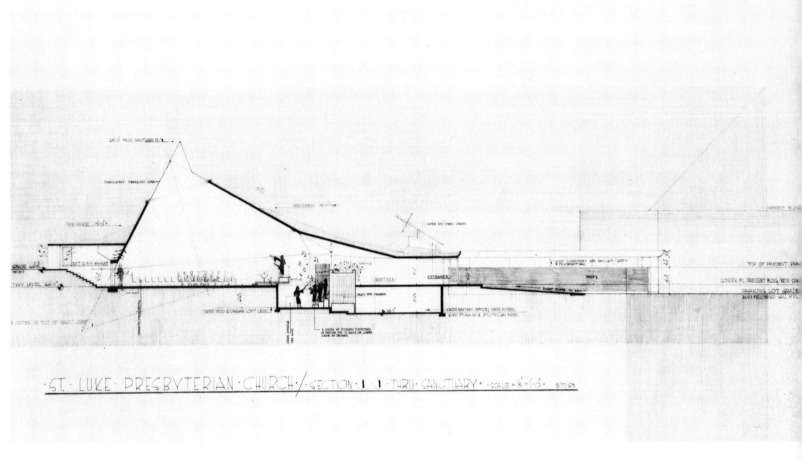

ST · LUKE · PRESBYTERIAN · CHURCH / SECTION · I - I · THRU · SANCTUARY · SCALE = ⅛" = 1'-0" · 3/22/68

St. Luke Presbyterian Church
Minnetonka, Minnesota      1968
Section through sanctuary,
colored pencil on paper
Courtesy Arthur A. Carrara, Architect

# JOHN H. HOWE (BORN 1915)

Raised in Evanston, Illinois, John H. Howe was exposed to the work of Frank Lloyd Wright and his philosophy at an early age. In 1932, immediately after graduation from high school, he joined the Taliesin Fellowship as one of the twenty charter members the year it was founded by Mr. and Mrs. Frank Lloyd Wright. In 1937 John Howe became Wright's chief draftsman and served in that capacity for twenty-seven years, working on such well-known projects as Herbert Jacobs first residence of 1936, the 1936 Johnson Wax Company buildings, Edgar Kaufmann's "Fallingwater" of 1935, and over forty Usonian houses. Many of the soft colored pencil renderings used for presentation were completed by Howe, as were drawings for the special issues of *Architectural Forum* showing the work of Wright in 1938 and 1948.

After Wright's death, John Howe began his independent work, first as a member of the Taliesin Associated Architects and since 1967 in his own office in Minneapolis, Minnesota. After having worked with Wright for such a long period of time, Howe's practice follows the principles of an organic architecture—that the building is in harmony with its site, that it naturally expresses its purpose, and that it is built according to the nature of the materials and the construction process. Wright stated that "the land is the beginning of architecture" and it is on this premise that John Howe bases his work.

As well as maintaining his architectural practice, Howe has lectured throughout the United States and was visiting professor in architecture at Nihon University in Japan for the school year 1975.

HOUSE FOR M
WAYZATA, MINNESOTA
JOHN H. HOWE ARCHIT

242

George R. Johnson Residence
Wayzata, Minnesota    1963
Pencil and ink on paper
23⅝ × 36½" (60 × 93 cm)
Courtesy John H. Howe, Architect

MRS. GEORGE R. JOHNSON

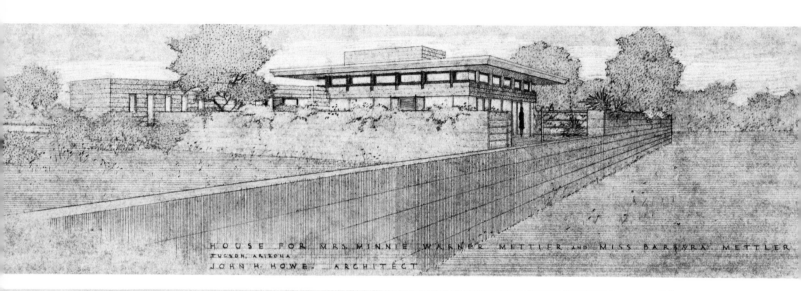

**244**   Mrs. Minnie Warner and Miss Barbara
Mettler Residence Project
Tucson, Arizona     1968
Pencil on paper
14¼ × 36″ (36 × 91 cm)
Courtesy John H. Howe, Architect

Dr. Robert Goodale Residence
Excelsior, Minnesota     1969
Pencil and ink on paper
15½ × 28½″ (39 × 72 cm)
Courtesy John H. Howe, Architect

VIEW FROM NORTHWEST

PROPOSED MOTOR HOTEL FOR HILLEREN ASSOCIATES

ROCHESTER MINNESOTA

JOHN H. HOWE AND ASSOCIATES, ARCHITECTS, MINNEAPOLIS, MINN.

245

Motor hotel for Hilleren Associates
(Project)
Rochester, Minnesota    1970
Pencil and ink on paper
30 × 24″ (76 × 61 cm)
Courtesy John H. Howe, Architect

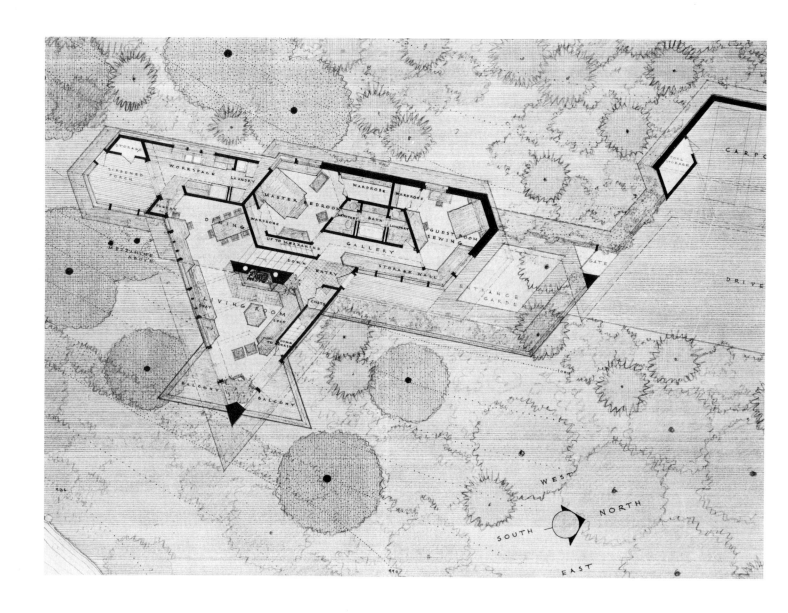

246     "Woodhome," John H. Howe Residence
        Burnsville, Minnesota    1971
        Pencil and ink on paper
        29½ × 40" (75 × 102 cm)
        Courtesy John H. Howe, Architect

"Woodhome," John H. Howe Residence
Burnsville, Minnesota    1971
Pencil and ink on paper
Courtesy John H. Howe, Architect

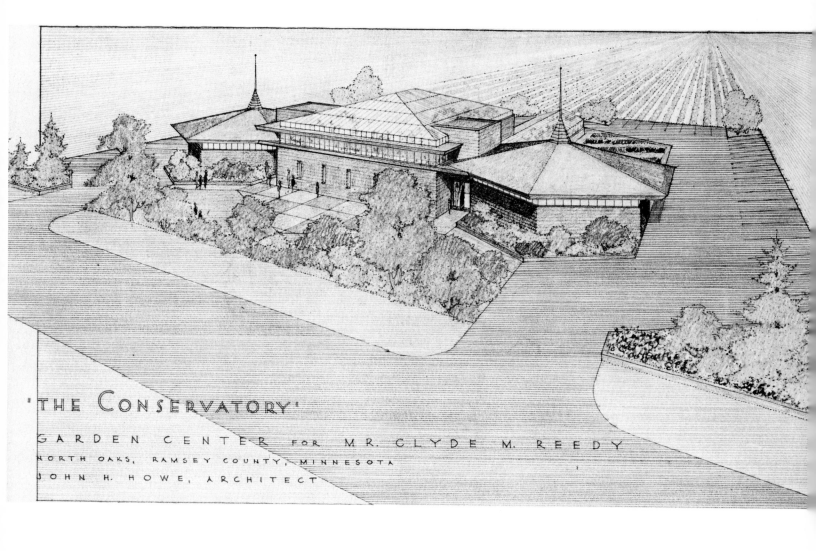

"THE CONSERVATORY"

GARDEN CENTER FOR MR. CLYDE M. REEDY
NORTH OAKS, RAMSEY COUNTY, MINNESOTA
JOHN H. HOWE, ARCHITECT

**248**   "The Conservatory" (Project)
Garden Center for Clyde M. Reedy
North Oaks, Minnesota     1974
Pencil and ink on paper
14¾ × 24¾" (38 × 63 cm)
Courtesy John H. Howe, Architect

VIEW FROM THE SOUTHEAST

TAIGA TOFT COMMUNE HOUSE
ROGERS MINNESOTA
JOHN H HOWE, ARCHITECT

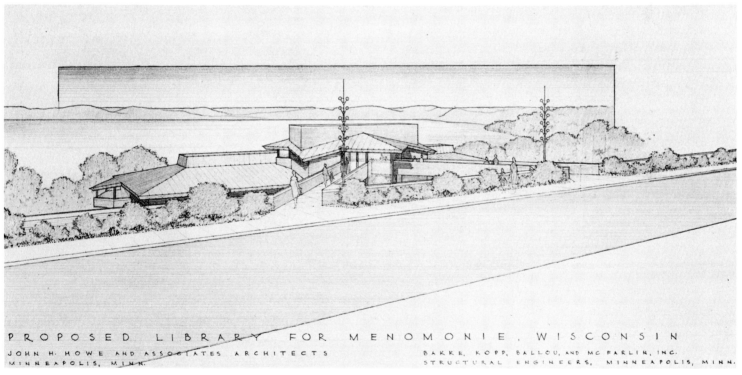

PROPOSED LIBRARY FOR MENOMONIE, WISCONSIN
JOHN H. HOWE AND ASSOCIATES ARCHITECTS            BAKKE, KOPP, BALLOU, AND MC FARLIN, INC.
MINNEAPOLIS, MINN.                                STRUCTURAL ENGINEERS, MINNEAPOLIS, MINN.

Taiga Toft Commune House
Rogers, Minnesota    1974
Pencil and ink on paper
15 × 37" (38 × 94 cm)
Courtesy John H. Howe, Architect

Proposed library for
Menominee, Wisconsin    1976
Pencil and ink on paper
17¼ × 29½" (44 × 75 cm)
Courtesy John H. Howe, Architect

# TALIESIN ASSOCIATED ARCHITECTS
## FOUNDED 1959

Taliesin Associated Architects is the architectural office of the Frank Lloyd Wright Foundation, established by the men and women trained by Frank Lloyd Wright to continue his design philosophy. In addition to completing works of Frank Lloyd Wright's not executed during his lifetime, the firm has designed over two hundred buildings in the United States and abroad.

Commissions of Taliesin Associated Architects have included commercial and residential work, school buildings, churches, theaters, city planning, highway and bridge design, parks and land development and restoration, as well as furniture, fabrics, and accessories for individual commissions and for commercial production.

Taliesin Associated Architects, as part of the Frank Lloyd Wright Foundation, is governed by its Board of Directors. Mrs. Frank Lloyd Wright, who reviews all architectural designs and works with the architects on color selections and interior designs, is president of the board. Other directors include William Wesley Peters, vice president, chief architect and planner; John DeKoven Hill, secretary; Richard Carney, treasurer; Iovanna Lloyd Wright Schiffner; and Joseph F. Rorke, M.D.

The foundation supports the Frank Lloyd Wright School of Architecture founded by Mr. and Mrs. Wright in 1932. The school maintains a year-round schedule for selected students, who receive training as apprentices in the drafting room, in regularly appointed classes, and in assigned work on construction needed to extend and maintain the buildings at Taliesin and Taliesin West.

The main office of the Frank Lloyd Wright Foundation is at Taliesin West in Scottsdale, Arizona, and in the summer months, at Taliesin in Spring Green, Wisconsin. The foundation also has representatives in San Francisco, Denver, and New York.

New pavilion for Belmont Park
(For the New York Racing Association, Inc.)
Long Island, New York    1964
William Wesley Peters, Project Architect
Colored pencil on tracing paper
22 × 29¾" (56 × 76 cm)
Courtesy Taliesin Associated Architects of
The Frank Lloyd Wright Foundation

252    Mr. & Mrs. Norman Lykes Residence
Phoenix, Arizona    1959
Preliminary Design, Frank Lloyd Wright
John Rattenbury, Project Architect
Colored pencil on tracing paper
15½ × 31½″ (39 × 80 cm)
Courtesy Taliesin Associated Architects of
The Frank Lloyd Wright Foundation

Mr. & Mrs. Norman Lykes Residence
Phoenix, Arizona    1959
Preliminary Design, Frank Lloyd Wright
John Rattenbury, Project Architect
Courtesy Taliesin Associated Architects of
The Frank Lloyd Wright Foundation

253

254    Mr. & Mrs. Lee Paulsel Residence
Benbrook, Texas    1965
John DeKoven Hill, Architect
Colored pencil on tracing paper
23⅛ × 35⅝" (59 × 90 cm)
Courtesy Taliesin Associated Architects of
The Frank Lloyd Wright Foundation

Lincoln Income Life Insurance Company
Louisville, Kentucky     1960
William Wesley Peters, Project Architect
Kenneth Lockhart, Architect; Kelly Oliver,
Supervising Architect
Courtesy Taliesin Associated Architects of
The Frank Lloyd Wright Foundation

256  Administration Building
     Rocky Mountain National Park,
     Colorado    1966
     Edmond Thomas Casey, Architect
     Colored pencil on tracing paper
     18¼ × 36⅛" (46 × 92 cm)
     Courtesy Taliesin Associated Architects of
     The Frank Lloyd Wright Foundation

VIEW FROM THE SOUTHEAST

257

Mr. & Mrs. Daniel Kessler Residence
Maplewood, New Jersey    1968
John Rattenbury, Architect
Courtesy Taliesin Associated Architects of
The Frank Lloyd Wright Foundation

ST. MARY'S CHURCH ALMA, MICHIGAN

**258**  St. Mary's Church
Alma, Michigan    1970
William Wesley Peters, Architect
Colored pencil on tracing paper
29¼ × 35½" (74 × 93 cm)
Courtesy Taliesin Associated Architects of
The Frank Lloyd Wright Foundation

St. Mary's Church
Alma, Michigan    1970
William Wesley Peters, Architect
Colored pencil on tracing paper
33 × 31" (84 × 79 cm)
Courtesy Taliesin Associated Architects of
The Frank Lloyd Wright Foundation

260     Villa on the Caspian (For Her Imperial
Highness Princess Shams Pahlavi)
Chalus, Iran     1970
William Wesley Peters, Chief Architect
Mrs. Frank Lloyd Wright, Interior Design
E. T. Casey, Iranian Representative
Nezam Amery, Iranian Architect Associated
Courtesy Taliesin Associated Architects of
The Frank Lloyd Wright Foundation

Eugenia Van Wezel Performing Arts Theatre
Sarasota, Florida    1970
William Wesley Peters, Project Architect
Vernon D. Swaback, Architect
Kenneth B. Lockhart, Architect
Courtesy Taliesin Associated Architects of
The Frank Lloyd Wright Foundation

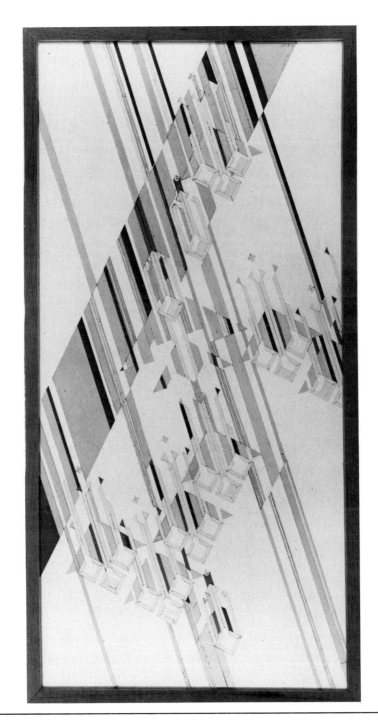

262

Columbine Abstraction    1971
Ling Po, Indira Berndtson
Clear and colored plexiglas in wood frame
Courtesy Taliesin Associated Architects of
The Frank Lloyd Wright Foundation

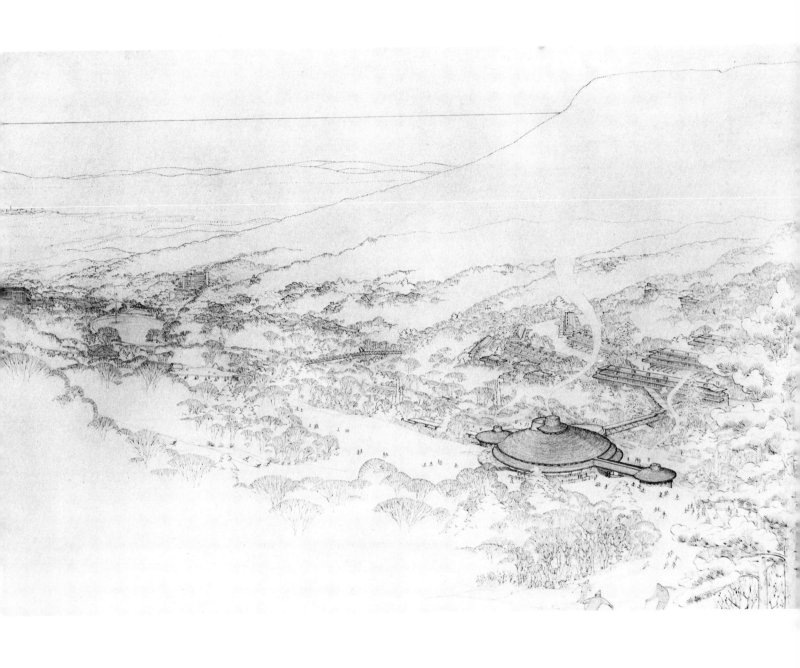

Mountain Run Ski Community
(For William McWilliams)
Shenandoah County, Virginia      1971
John Rattenbury, Architect
Colored pencil and ink on tracing paper
31⅞ × 47¾″ (81 × 121 cm)
Courtesy Taliesin Associated Architects of
The Frank Lloyd Wright Foundation

VAIL PASS STUDY FOR THE DIVISION OF HIGHWAYS, STATE OF COLORADO
THE FRANK LLOYD WRIGHT FOUNDATION, CHARLES MONTOOTH, ARCHITECT
FOR BARTON, STODDARD, MILHOLLIN & HIGGINS

STRUCTURE ON HILLSIDE ABOVE EAST VAIL

264    I-70 Vail Pass, Colorado    1971
(For the Division of Highways)
Charles Montooth, Architect
Segmental precast concrete bridge
concept, colored pencil on tracing paper
23 × 36″ (58 × 91 cm)
Courtesy Taliesin Associated Architects of
The Frank Lloyd Wright Foundation

"Ponds and Pines" Island Cottage
Lake Notre Dame, Southern Pines,
North Carolina    1973
David Elgin Dodge, Architect
Colored pencil on tracing paper
25½ × 36" (65 × 91 cm)
Courtesy Taliesin Associated Architects of
The Frank Lloyd Wright Foundation

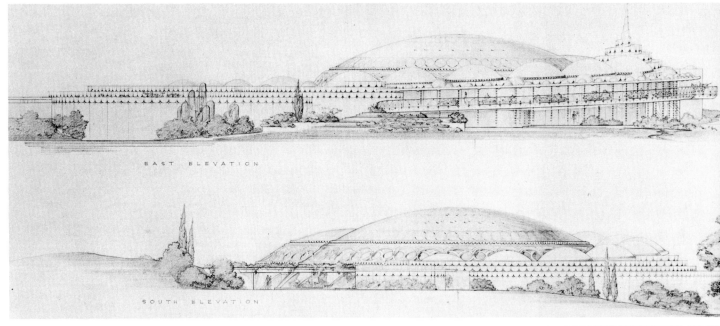

266

Top
Palace for Her Royal Highness Princess
Shams Pahlavi
Mehr-Dasht, Iran     1973
William Wesley Peters, Chief Architect
Mrs. Frank Lloyd Wright, Interior Design
E. T. Casey, Iranian Representative
Nezam Amery, Iranian Architect Associated
Colored pencil on tracing paper
17¾ × 37½" (45 × 95 cm)
Courtesy Taliesin Associated Architects of
The Frank Lloyd Wright Foundation

Bottom
Palace for Her Royal Highness Princess
Shams Pahlavi
Mehr-Dasht, Iran     1973
William Wesley Peters, Chief Architect
Mrs. Frank Lloyd Wright, Interior Design
E. T. Casey, Iranian Representative
Nezam Amery, Iranian Architect Associated
Colored pencil on tracing paper
17¾ × 39" (45 × 99 cm)
Courtesy Taliesin Associated Architects of
The Frank Lloyd Wright Foundation

MAIN ENTRANCE

Palace for Her Royal Highness Princess
Shams Pahlavi
Mehr-Dasht, Iran    1973
William Wesley Peters, Chief Architect
Mrs. Frank Lloyd Wright, Interior Design
E. T. Casey, Iranian Representative
Nezam Amery, Iranian Architect Associated
Colored pencil on tracing paper
23 × 36″ (58 × 91 cm)
Courtesy Taliesin Associated Architects of
The Frank Lloyd Wright Foundation

# WILLIAM P. WENZLER (BORN 1929)

Born in Milwaukee, Wisconsin, in 1929, William P. Wenzler began his architectural education at the University of Wisconsin, Milwaukee, and completed his studies at the University of Illinois. He apprenticed from 1952 to 1955 in the Milwaukee firm of Brust & Brust and in 1955 he opened his own office. His early work quickly gained recognition, particularly the shell structures of St. Edmonds' Episcopal Church of 1957 and Zion Lutheran Church of 1958, both in the Milwaukee area.

Wenzler received the Francis J. Plym Fellowship from the University of Illinois in 1958 that allowed for travel to Europe for six months. Upon his return, his practice continued to draw attention in the United States and abroad, with publication of his work in a number of European architectural periodicals. The strongly adhered-to principles of Wenzler's practice are the integration of the architectural aesthetic with the beauty of the structure and an emphasis on the natural form of materials, the construction method, and respect for human scale in the built environment. The scope of Wenzler's work in residential design, industrial buildings, office buildings, schools, churches, and adaptive reuse and planning broadly expresses the design premise of the firm. The Nickoll and Gerlach residences utilize different materials, each true to themselves in the nature of construction and each providing totally individual answers to a common architectural problem. At the other end of the scale is the Inland Steel Products Company factory building that utilizes the nature and technology of a machine product.

The Lutheran Social Services office building offers protection with its curved corners, ensuring a sense of privacy to the organization's clients, while the Calvary Baptist Church outwardly expresses the traditional building forms of the Cameroons and reinforces the congregation's black heritage.

Other principal members of the firm of William Wenzler and Associates are David F. Brandt, professional engineer, and James S. McClintock, architect.

Nickoll Residence
Fox Point, Wisconsin    1961
Courtesy William Wenzler and Associates,
Architects

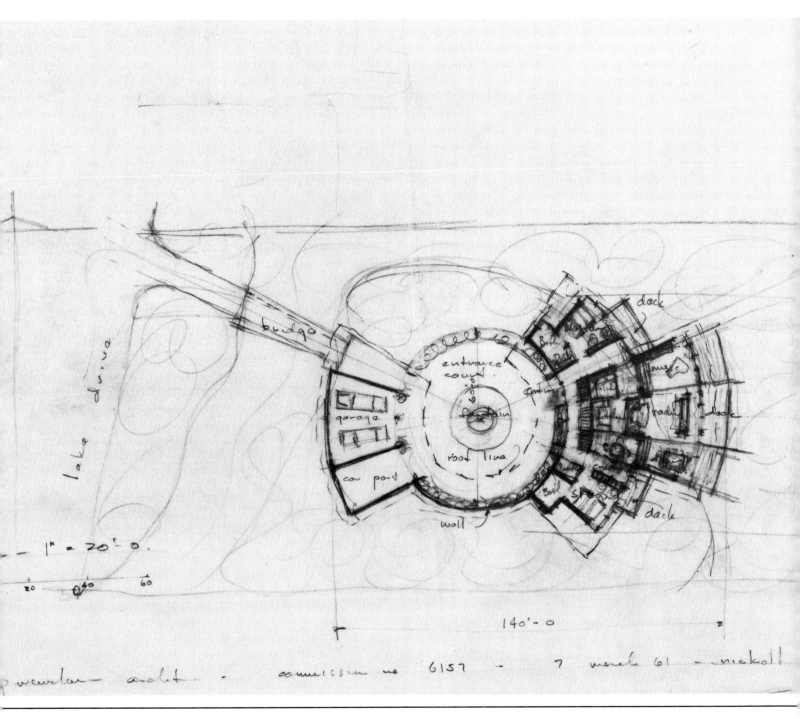

Within the drawing, handwritten labels: bridge, lake drive, garage, car port, entrance court, fountain, roof line, wall, music, study, deck

1" = 20'-0.

20  0  40  60

140'-0

commission no 6157  —  7 march 61  —  nickoll

vernacular — archt.

Nickoll Residence
Fox Point, Wisconsin    1961
Pencil on tracing paper
12 × 16⅝" (31 × 42 cm)
Courtesy William Wenzler and Associates,
Architects

270   Inland Steel Products Company Factory
      Milwaukee, Wisconsin    1964
      Courtesy William Wenzler and Associates,
      Architects

Calvary Baptist Church
Milwaukee, Wisconsin    1966
Courtesy William Wenzler and Associates,
Architects

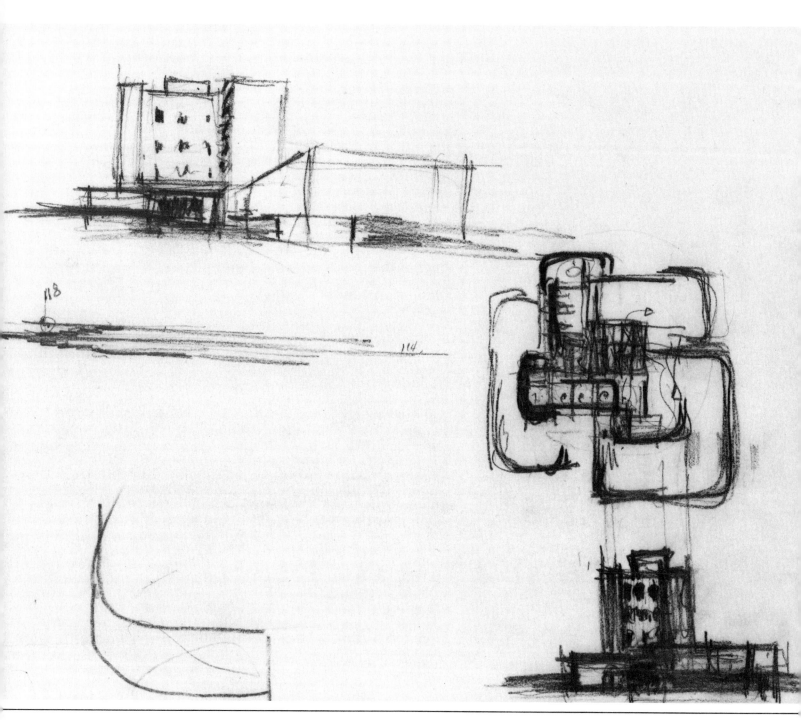

272    Office building for Lutheran Social Services
       of Wisconsin and Upper Michigan
       Milwaukee, Wisconsin    1965
       Pencil on tracing paper
       10½ × 16½" (27 × 42 cm)
       Courtesy William Wenzler and Associates,
       Architects

Office building for Lutheran Social Services
of Wisconsin and Upper Michigan
Milwaukee, Wisconsin    1965
Courtesy William Wenzler and Associates,
Architects

**274** Gerlach Residence
Elm Grove, Wisconsin    1965
Courtesy William Wenzler and Associates,
Architects

Gerlach Residence
Elm Grove, Wisconsin
Courtesy William Wenzler and Associates,
Architects

# HERB GREENE (BORN 1929)

Born in Oneonta, New York, Herb Greene became a student of Bruce Goff at the University of Oklahoma. This led to a professional association. The imagination and versatility of Herb Greene's architecture can be seen in his individual houses, projects for low-cost housing, commercial buildings, multi-use facilities, and projects for urban renovation. In addition to practicing architecture throughout the United States, Greene is both artist and teacher; he has been a professor of architecture at the University of Kentucky since 1964. His numerous articles and books dealing with the function of art and architecture in today's society have approached both practical and theoretical issues, including such topics as the failure of public housing projects, commercial buildings along major transportation routes, society's perception of architectural images, and the processes of organic design which Greene himself advocates.

276

Residence Project    1955
Colored pencil on sepia print
11⅜ × 36" (29 × 91 cm)
Courtesy Herb Greene, Architect

WEST   ELEVATION

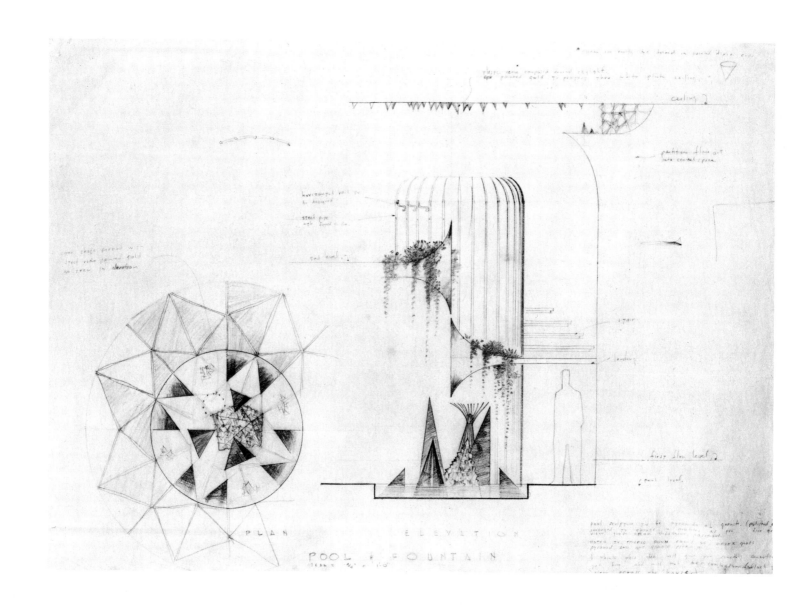

Mr. & Mrs. John Joyce Residence
Snyder, Oklahoma    1958-1960
Pool and fountain, colored pencil
on paper
21 × 29¼" (53 × 74 cm)
Courtesy Herb Greene, Architect

Herb Greene Residence
Norman, Oklahoma    1960-1961
Courtesy Herb Greene, Architect

280    Cunningham Residence
Oklahoma City, Oklahoma   1963
Colored pencil on sepia print
12½ × 28¾" (32 × 73 cm)
Courtesy Herb Greene, Architect

Cunningham Residence
Oklahoma City, Oklahoma     1963
Courtesy Herb Greene, Architect

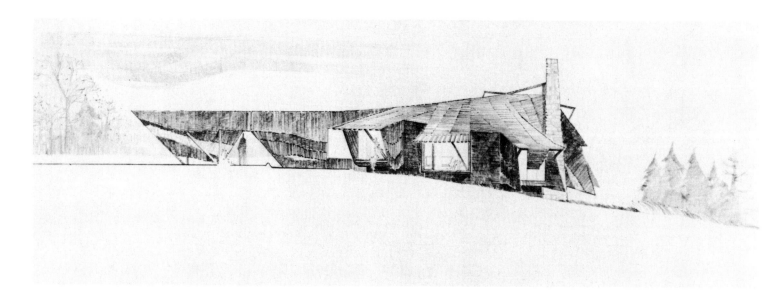

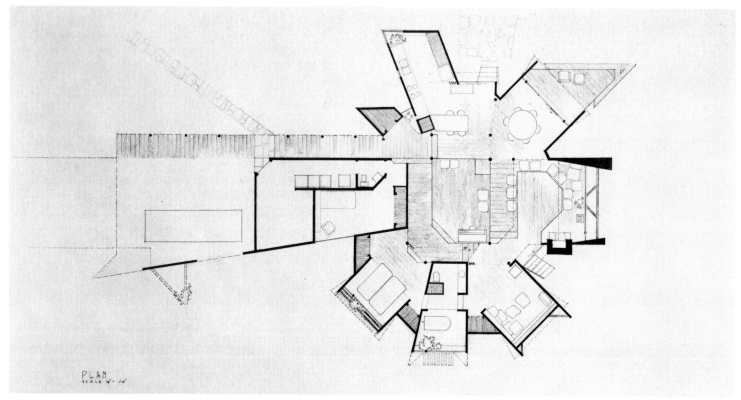

282  House for April Rooks and Lou Deluca
Lawrenceburg, Kentucky    1972
Pencil on paper
16¾ × 36″ (43 × 91 cm)
Courtesy Herb Greene, Architect

House for April Rooks and Lou Deluca
Lawrenceburg, Kentucky    1972
Pencil on paper
22½ × 36″ (57 × 91 cm)
Courtesy Herb Greene, Architect

Urban Study    1976-1977
Colored pencil on sepia print
17½ × 36″ (45 × 91 cm)
Courtesy Herb Greene, Architect

283

# THOMAS OLSON (BORN 1930)

Thomas Olson was born and raised in the Hastings, Minnesota, area. Following graduation from high school, he enlisted in the Minnesota National Guard, and was soon activated to full duty for service during the Korean War. Following discharge from the service, Olson applied for study in architecture with Frank Lloyd Wright and began his architectural training with the Taliesin Fellowship in the fall of 1952. During his apprenticeship period he supervised construction of the William P. Boswell Residence in 1957 in Cincinnati, Ohio, and the Dr. George Albin Residence in 1958 in Bakersfield, California.

Olson left the Taliesin Fellowship in 1961 to return to Hastings to manage the family business. His own practice of architecture began in 1962 with designs for the Hoffman Residence, which still remains to be built. His practice to date has not been extensive, but other projects and executed works in the Minneapolis-St. Paul area worth noting include the Niederkorn Residence of 1969, the David G. Smith Residence of 1976, and the Hale Residence of 1977.

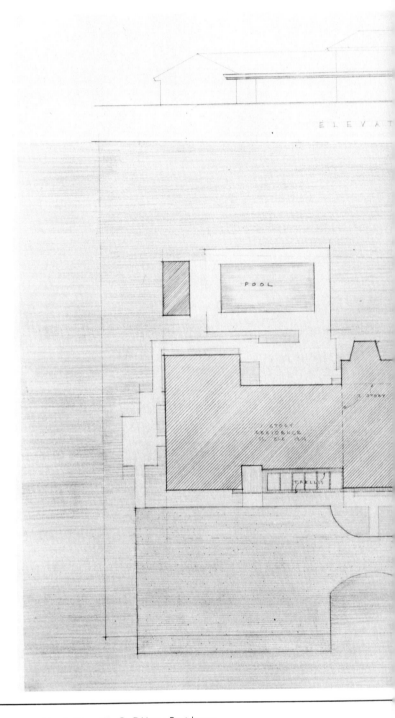

Mr. & Mrs. W. C. D'Arcy Residence
Hobe Sound, Florida
Colored pencil on tracing paper
35 × 39" (89 × 99 cm)
Courtesy Thomas Olson

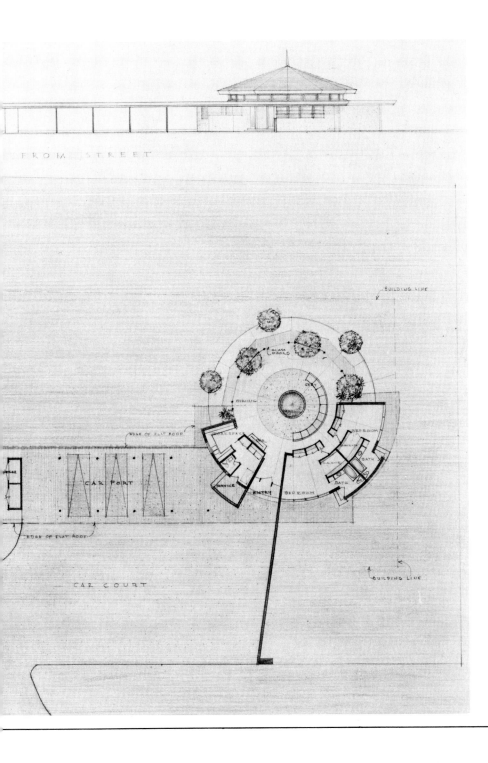

FROM STREET

BUILDING LINE

GLASS DOORS

DINING

LIVING SPACE

BEDROOM

EDGE OF FLAT ROOF

BATH

BATH

SERVICE

CAR PORT

ENTRY    BEDROOM

EDGE OF FLAT ROOF

CAR COURT

BUILDING LINE

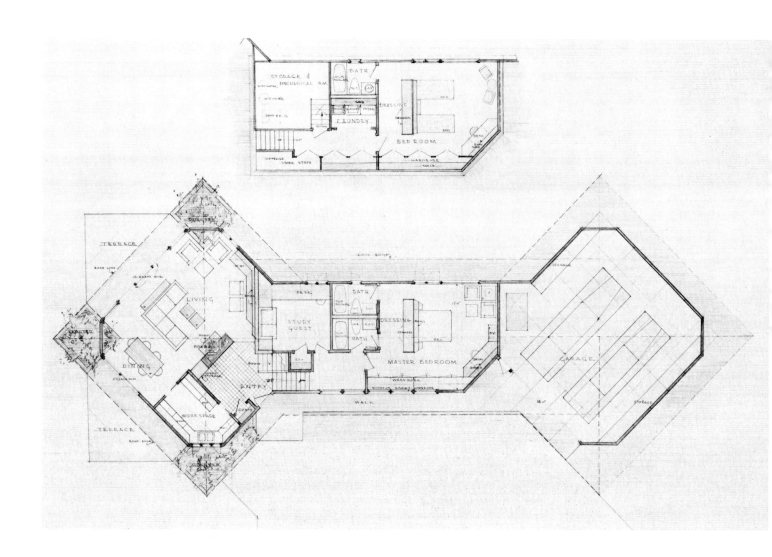

Private residence near Hastings,
Minnesota    1976
Colored pencil on paper
23⅞ × 36″ (61 × 91 cm)
Courtesy Thomas Olson

Private residence near Hastings,
Minnesota    1976
Courtesy Thomas Olson

# MICHAEL P. JOHNSON (BORN 1938)

Michael P. Johnson was born and raised in Milwaukee, Wisconsin. Upon graduation from high school, he studied education briefly at Stout State University and then switched to engineering at the University of Wisconsin, Milwaukee. Johnson's architectural training began in the office of Mark Pfaller, Architect, in 1958. After two years in Pfaller's office, he left the firm to join Francis Gurda and in 1961 went to work with William P. Wenzler, Architect. There Johnson worked on such projects as the Nickoll Residence of 1961, Inland Steel Products Company factory building of 1964, and the Lutheran Social Services office building of 1965.

In 1967, Michael Johnson left the Wenzler firm and opened his own design studio in Colgate, Wisconsin. At this time, Johnson's designs began to express more the architectural ideas of his inspirational mentor, Bruce Goff. His residential designs explored uncommon shapes and spaces in the rather traditional Milwaukee region. One project, Sconfinato, gave Johnson the opportunity for total design control. A rural subdivision, Sconfinato represents Johnson's search for harmony between buildings and nature. Of note at Sconfinato are the Robert C. Caldart Residence (scheme 2) of 1969, the Paul Kasbohm Residence of 1970, the Clyde Monda Residence of 1970, and the Russell Kagan Residence of 1972.

In 1976, Johnson moved to New River, Arizona, where he now practices design. His work has been published in *L'Architettura Cronache e Storia* in Italy and in *L'Architecture d'aujourd'hui* in France. Exhibitions of his work have been shown at Carroll College in Wisconsin and George Washington University. He has presented lectures on his design philosophy at Calton University in Canada, the University of Wisconsin, Milwaukee, and the Layton School of Art in Milwaukee.

Robert Caldart Residence I
Brookfield, Wisconsin    1967
Pencil on tracing paper
24 × 36" (61 × 91 cm)
Courtesy Michael P. Johnson

290    Robert Caldart Residence II
       Town of Erin, Wisconsin   1969
       Pencil on tracing paper
       24 × 36″ (61 × 91 cm)
       Courtesy Michael P. Johnson

Russell Kagan Residence I
Town of Erin, Wisconsin   1970
Pencil on tracing paper
24 × 36" (61 × 91 cm)
Courtesy Michael P. Johnson

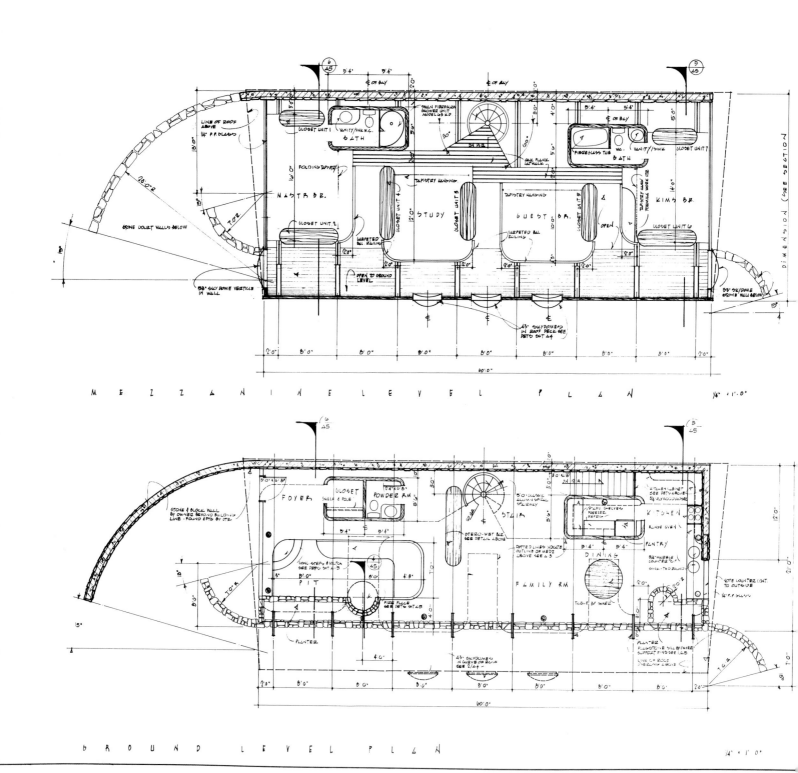

292   Russell Kagan Residence II
      Town of Erin, Wisconsin    1972
      Ink and pencil on tracing paper
      24 × 36" (61 × 91 cm)
      Courtesy Michael P. Johnson

      Russell Kagan Residence II
      Town of Erin, Wisconsin    1972
      Pencil on tracing paper
      24 × 36" (61 × 91 cm)
      Courtesy Michael P. Johnson

Russell Kagan Residence II
Town of Erin, Wisconsin     1972
Pencil on tracing paper
24 × 36″ (61 × 91 cm)
Courtesy Michael P. Johnson

# WILLIAM P. BRUDER (BORN 1946)

William P. Bruder was born in Milwaukee, Wisconsin, in 1946. He was educated at the University of Wisconsin where he received a Bachelor of Fine Arts degree in sculpture. Bruder apprenticed in the firms of William Wenzler, Michael P. Johnson, Paolo Soleri, Gunnar Birkerts, and Goodwin Associates, beginning his own private practice in 1974 in New River, Arizona.

Bruder's young office has already produced no less than forty design projects, including his own home and studio of 1975, which received an award of excellence from *Architectural Record* magazine in 1977. The J. L. Bammerlin Postal Federal Credit Union of 1974 in Phoenix received an Illuminating Engineering Society award of merit for Bruder's lighting design, and his Calloway Cabin of 1973 in Pine River, Arizona, was awarded first honors in 1977 by the American Plywood Association's annual design competition. Bruder has lectured and written on architecture that is in harmony with the environment. This philosophy is reflected consistently in his designs, ranging from small patio additions and desert dwellings to commercial office buildings.

William P. Bruder Residence
Black Canyon Stage, New River, Arizona
Courtesy William Bruder, Architect

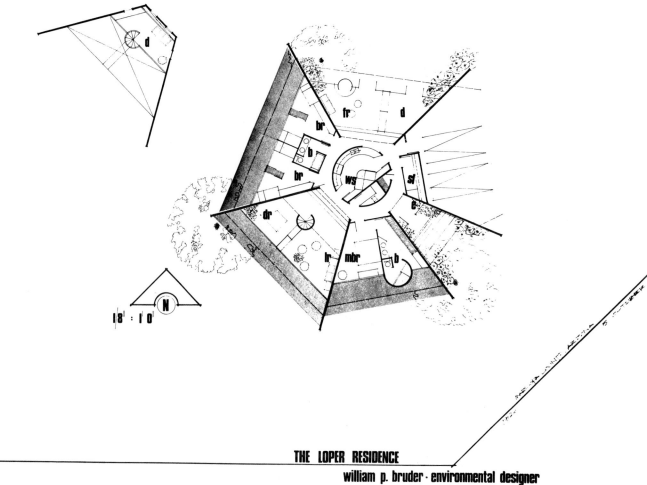

THE LOPER RESIDENCE
william p. bruder · environmental designer

296   Loper Residence
Chandler, Arizona    1973
Ink on tracing paper
24 × 36" (61 × 91 cm)
Courtesy William Bruder, Architect

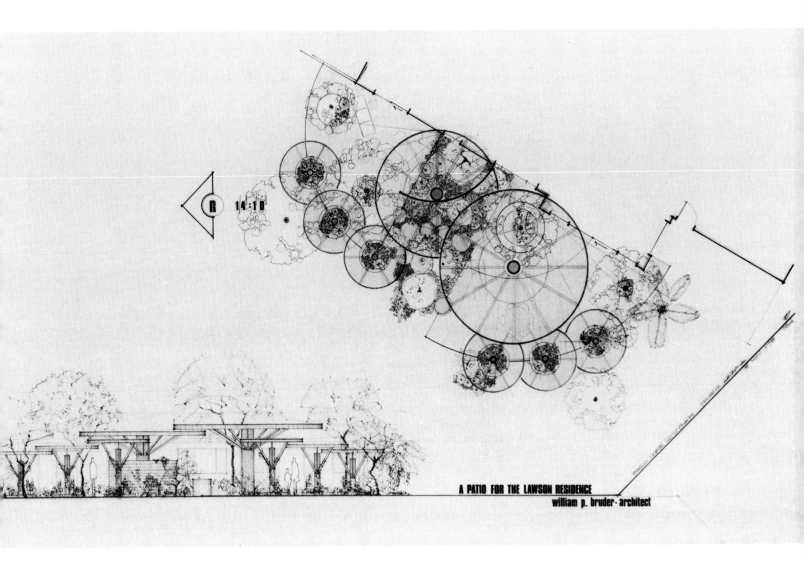

A PATIO FOR THE LAWSON RESIDENCE
william p. bruder · architect

Lawson Residence
Phoenix, Arizona    1974
Ink on tracing paper
24 × 36″ (61 × 91 cm)
Courtesy William Bruder, Architect

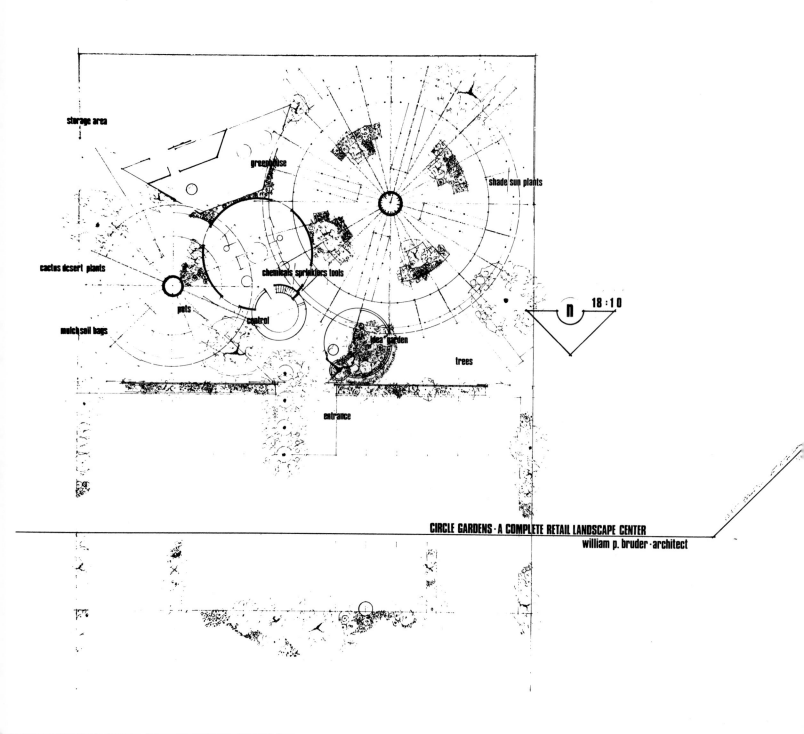

storage area

greenhouse

shade sun plants

cactus desert plants

chemicals sprinklers tools

pots

control

mulch soil bags

idea garden

trees

entrance

N   18:10

CIRCLE GARDENS · A COMPLETE RETAIL LANDSCAPE CENTER

william p. bruder · architect

298    Circle Gardens: A Complete Retail
       Landscape Center
       Mesa, Arizona    1976
       Ink on tracing paper
       24 × 36″ (61 × 91 cm)
       Courtesy William Bruder, Architect

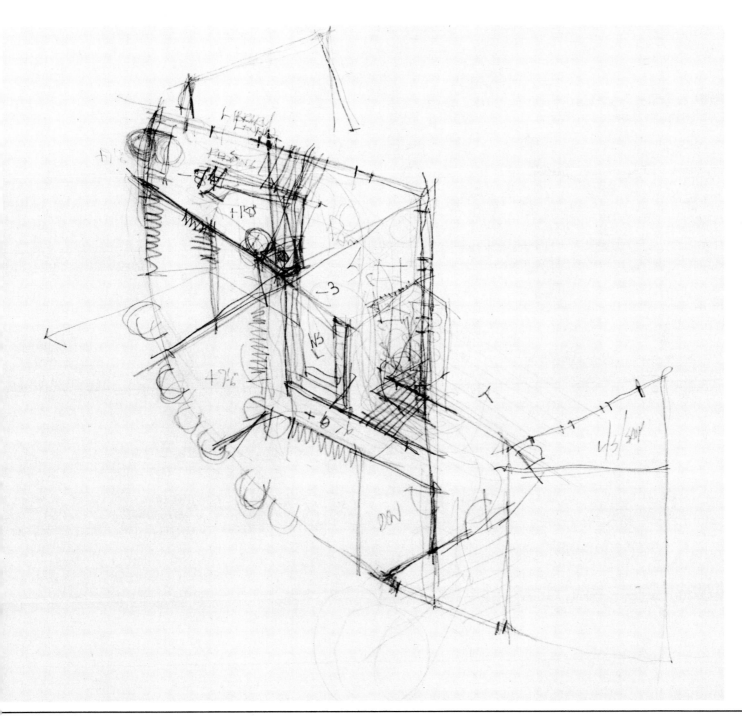

Peters Residence
Mesa, Arizona    1977
Pencil on tracing paper
12 × 21″ (31 × 53 cm)
Courtesy William Bruder, Architect

Brooks, H. Allen. *The Prairie School: Frank Lloyd Wright and His Midwest Contemporaries.* Toronto and Buffalo: University of Toronto Press, 1972.

————. "Percy Dwight Bentley at La Crosse." *The Prairie School Review* 9, no. 3 (Third Quarter, 1972).

Carrara, Arthur A. *A Flexagon of Structure and Design.* Milwaukee: Milwaukee Art Center, 1960

Chappell, Sally Anderson. "Barry Byrne, Architect: His Formative Years." *The Prairie School Review* 3, no. 4 (Fourth Quarter, 1966).

Condit, Carl W. *The Chicago School of Architecture: A History of Commercial and Public Building in the Chicago Area 1875–1925.* Chicago and London: The University of Chicago Press, 1964.

Connely, Willard. *Louis Sullivan: The Shaping of American Architecture.* New York: Horizon Press, 1956.

Delong, David. *The Architecture of Bruce Goff; Buildings and Projects; 1916-1974.* New York: Garland, 1976.

Gebhard, David. "Purcell and Elmslie—Architects." *The Prairie School Review* 2, no. 1 (First Quarter, 1965).

————, and von Breton, Harriet. *Lloyd Wright, Architect: 20th-Century Architecture in an Organic Exhibition.* Santa Barbara, Calif.: The Standard Printing Co., 1971.

Griggs, Joseph. "Alfonso Iannelli: The Prairie Spirit in Sculpture." *The Prairie School Review* 2, no. 4 (Fourth Quarter, 1965).

Hitchcock, Henry-Russell. *In the Nature of Materials.* New York: Duell, Sloan and Pearce, 1942.

————. *The Architecture of H.H. Richardson and His Times.* Hamden, Conn.: Archon Books, 1961.

Hoffman, Donald L. "The Brief Career of a Sullivan Apprentice: Parker N. Berry." *The Prairie School Review* 4, no. 1 (First Quarter, 1967).

Howe, John H. "Works of J. H. Howe." *Kenchiku Bunka* (Japan), no. 394 (November 1975).

Kalec, Donald. "The Prairie School Furniture." *The Prairie School Press* 1, no. 4 (Fourth Quarter, 1964).

Kaufmann, Edgar, Jr., *The Rise of an American Architecture.* New York: Praeger Publishers (in association with the Metropolitan Museum of Art), 1970.

Kosta, Robert. "Bruce Goff and the New Tradition." *The Prairie School Review* 3, no. 2 (Second Quarter, 1970).

————. "Frank Lloyd Wright in Japan." *The Prairie School Review* 3, no. 3 (Third Quarter, 1966).

Makinson, Randall L. "Greene and Greene: The Gamble House." *The Prairie School Review* 5, no. 4 (Fourth Quarter, 1968).

————. *A Guide to the Work of Greene and Greene.* Salt Lake City: Peregrine Smith, 1974.

McCoy, Robert E. "Rock Crest/Rock Glen: Prairie Planning in Iowa." *The Prairie School Review* 5, no. 3 (Third Quarter, 1968).

O'Gorman, James F. *H.H. Richardson and His Office: Selected Drawings.* Boston: Godine, 1974.

————. *The Architecture of Frank Furness.* Philadelphia: Philadelphia Museum of Art, 1973.

Powell, Eileen Alt, and Sazama, Cindy. *Sconfinato: A Photo Essay.* Colgate, Wisc., undated.

Sullivan, Louis H. *The Autobiography of an Idea.* New York: Dover Publications, Inc., 1956.

Wright, Frank Lloyd. *An Autobiography.* New York: Longmans, Green and Company, 1932.

————. *The Future of Architecture.* New York: Horizon Press, 1953.

300

# PHOTOGRAPHY CREDITS

Unless otherwise noted by page number below or in the text captions, photography courtesy P. Richard Eells.

The Art Institute of Chicago: 26, 37, 44-45, 49, 50, 58, 68-69, 77, 116-119, 159

Avery Library, Columbia University: 23, 26, 29, 36-37, 53

Big Cedar Studios: 268

Richard W. Bock Collection, Greenville College: 164-167

Arthur A. Carrara: 233

Robert A. Dorn: 270, 273

Elvehjem Art Center: 67, 94

Alexandre Georges: 229

Hedrich-Blessing: 68, 100-101, 146-150, 271, 274

Thomas A. Heinz: 56, 157, 178

Houghton Library, Harvard University: 16-19, 21

S.C. Johnson & Son: 102-103

Koppes: 295

Thomas A. Olson: 287

David R. Phillips Studio: 20

Pohlman Studios: 269

Marvin Rand: 190-197

Cervin Robinson: 12-15

Brian A. Spencer: 31, 84

University Art Galleries, University of California, Santa Barbara: 198-199, 208

Jeffrey L. Wagner: 276, 280, 282

# INDEX

*Italics following an architect's name indicate illustrated works; following a city, italics indicate an illustration of work in that city.*

303

Edited by Sarah Bodine and Susan Davis
Designed by Jay Anning
Set in 10 point Futura Light

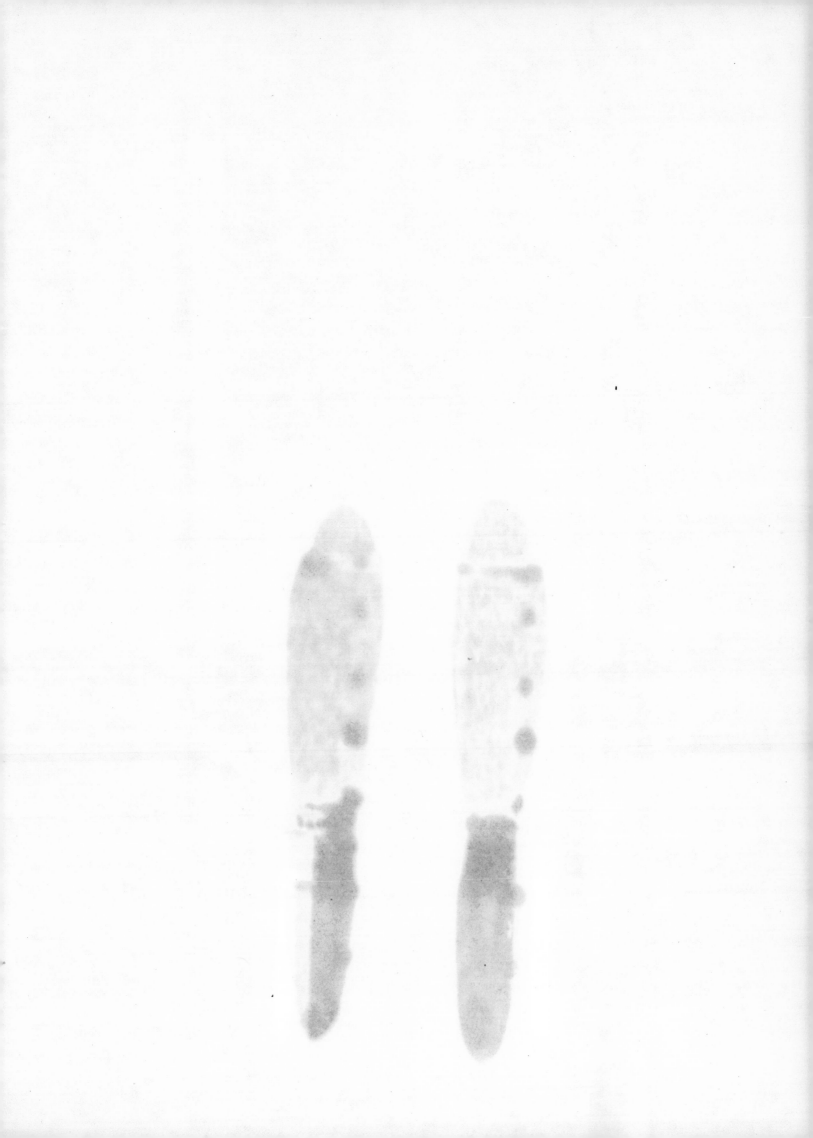